NOUVEAU POOR
OR HOW TO LIVE
BETTER ON LESS

NOUVEAU POOR

OR HOW TO LIVE
BETTER ON LESS

by

Barbara Griggs   &

Shirley Lowe

Illustrated by Tom Barling

HODDER AND STOUGHTON
LONDON SYDNEY AUCKLAND TORONTO

For Henri and Michael
without whom Nouveau Poverty
would be absolutely no fun at all.

FOREWORD
by
SHIRLEY CONRAN
author of SUPERWOMAN

Everybody in Britain today is noticeably poorer than they were. This book tells you how to live better in spite of it.

Everyone I know has had to cut down or give up long-cherished, hard-worked-for pleasures and luxuries. A few are smiling bravely, far more are glum, weighed down with the necessity for economy and desperately trying to work out how to practise it.

It's not fun being poor and I'm not going to pretend that it is, but if you can afford to buy this book or have the leisure to read it (being poor is incredibly time-consuming) then you're probably only poorer than you *were*. That's Nouveau Poor.

I was Nouveau Poor for years and years and I thought I had worked out most of the ways to have fun on the cheap (you can never have fun on nothing). This book contains not only all my old tricks but masses that I hadn't thought of and intend to put into practice immediately.

Nouveau Poor is a positive, realistic book. It points out that the best way to tighten your belt is to reduce your waistline. It reveals the silver lining of adversity, in which I firmly believe.

It doesn't pretend that women aren't frivolous, feminine, indulgent to their friends and their family and fond of good food and a comfortable home. It doesn't make brave resolutions based on weaving your own vest and hoeing your own goat or suggest opting out of the rat race.

Anyway, that solution is tougher than you may think. Look at all the people who opt back in again, man.

It does contain hard-headed advice from experts; down-to-earth practical suggestions from a couple of working wives and mothers who know what they are doing and paying for, and with whom I have worked for more years than any of us choose to remember.

Shirley and Barbara don't offer any magic way to save us £2,000 a year, but they do shower us with patterns, recipes, ideas, addresses, and information and tips from those who were not always so quotably rich, famous and successful as they are now. Economies tend to lose their sting if you know that they were first devised by Twiggy or Lady Harlech.

The most important thing about Nouveau Poor is the over-all attitude. It's not written in the spirit of 1940, in gum boots, through gritted teeth, but with wit and style and a marvellous zest for life. It's a book for those who want to waste nothing, live reasonably well in good surroundings, eat out and continue to entertain their friends to the point where they don't want to leave, without ending up in the bankruptcy court.

And the heartening thing about being Nouveau Poor *now* is that everyone is in the same boat. I christen this boat the H.M.S. Jones. May God bless her and all who sail in her.

SHIRLEY CONRAN 1976

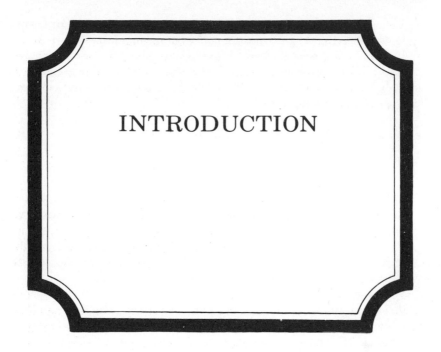

INTRODUCTION

We're Nouveau Poor and we don't mind a bit.

We're not sitting around moaning about the prices of smoked salmon — well, we always did like kippers better, anyway — because we think it's actually possible to live better on less money.

We've discovered that even if life can't be as materially easy as it was a few years ago, it can be every bit as enjoyable.

All you need is style. Nouveau Poor style.

We've researched. We've investigated. We've questioned. We've experimented. And we've picked some of the cleverest brains in the country — inspired amateurs as well as professional experts — to find out how to cut costs without cutting standards or becoming a penny-pinching bore.

We're certainly not suggesting you opt out for a life of homespun Self-Sufficiency; you at your loom while your man has another go at rigging up the solar heating system on the roof. Frankly, we'd rather buy a pot than throw one.

Nor do we intend to delve into the technicalities of such big-budget financial items as mortgages, central heating and insurance. They need whole books to themselves and other people have written them. Just turn to LOOK IT UP HERE on page to find out who, where and what they say.

We're concentrating on the lighthearted side of life, the pleasures that make it worth living. How to look good without spending a fortune on your face and hair and clothes; how to shop for the best and keep household bills down to a minimum; how to entertain your friends and do up your house without going bankrupt; how to eat out without guiltily spending a fistful of fivers.

How, in fact, to be Nouveau Poor and enjoy it.

* * *

Thank you to all the friends, colleagues and experts who allowed us to pick their brains. Thank you to Ruth Lasky for her invaluable work on the gardening chapter and her detailed research. Thank you to Mary Quant for her smashing Nouveau pattern. Thank you to Henri van der Zee for his down-to-earth contribution to the decorating chapter. Thank you to Chris Barham who took the pictures.

N.B. We've tried to avoid mentioning actual prices throughout the book because of their annoying tendency to keep on rising. Where we have done so it has either been unavoidable, or because it does at least give some idea of relative costs.

BARBARA GRIGGS AND SHIRLEY LOWE

CONTENTS

The Clothes File

The CLOTHES FILE

BE THIN

Be thin is the biggest single economy you can make in terms of dress. Preferably size ten, and if not, a well-proportioned size twelve. Anything over twelve and you either need a skilfully worked-out personal style to look good, or lots and lots of money, and better still, both.

If you're size ten, you can put on old jeans at the weekend, borrow your husband or son's ancient sweater, stick on a pair of gumboots for a family walk — and look a perfect smasher. If you're a well-fed size fourteen, you could invest in some Rive Gauche trousers, and a big beautiful Italian sweater from one of those pricey little boutiques, and some rather good boots — and you'll get there too. At a rather higher price. So if you're aiming to look good without going bankrupt, getting thin is, we're obliged to point out, the first and foremost move to make.

Work out the smallest size you can get to and maintain without turning into an agonising diet-bore. Then get there. And stay there. It'll save you a fortune in disguise-dressing.

How to?

Well, there's the classic Just-Eat-Less diet. Fashion P.R. Lindy Woodhead, who has glowy blonde good looks, and used to have a weight problem, decided to lose it for ever — and shed thirteen pounds in one month. Here's how:

"I had nothing at all for breakfast — just lemon in hot water. I always ate lunch because in my job it's difficult to duck it a lot of the time, and besides, I reckoned I burned it all off rushing around the rest of the day. I would start lunch with half a grapefruit, then roast chicken or grilled fish or steak, and a glass of dry white wine. No fat; fat is fattening, I'm

15

afraid. I tried to cut dinner down to zero unless we were going out — I mean, when you're going to bed soon after, it doesn't get burned up, does it, just lies there vegetating. No alcohol except for a little dry white wine — or a dry vermouth topped up with soda. Or champagne... And when I'm dieting I try to work like a beaver all the time, not just during the day but when I get home. I turn out cupboards and tidy drawers and replan our kitchen. It sounds agony but you have so much more energy when you're eating and drinking less..."

Another friend of ours, who loves food, swears by the twenty-four hour fast. Once in a while, she has a very light supper — then knocks off food and drink till supper-time the next day, and keeps that light too. No tea. No coffee. No nothing. Just lots and lots of Vichy or Malvern water — or straight out of the tap if she's feeling poor. A fantastic rest for the whole digestive system, which then gets to work with renewed vigour. The next day, she says, she only wants tiny meals, and three or four pounds simply fall off. (We don't need to point out that financially, this is a particularly rewarding diet...)

Then, since exercise helps you stay in shape, there's yoga; nothing like it according to Vidal Sassoon's ravishing dark-haired wife Beverley, for keeping a girl calm, radiant, and shapely: "I feel I'm even growing taller with constantly contracting and expanding my spine".

SO MUCH FOR THE BASIC YOU. NOW FOR WHAT YOU PUT ON IT.

The first and most important thing to realise is that there's no such thing as fashion — in the ghastly old dictatorial sense — any longer. There are fashions, and you can take your pick. There are Looks, and you choose the one that suits you. At a well-heeled London dinner-party this week, for instance, there might be one woman in a little black Jean Muir with pearls and polished court shoes; another in ethnic skirt and peasant blouse; another in side-slashed close-draped grey jersey; another in a plain gaberdine skirt, silk shirt and black suede boots. Not one of them would be *ipso facto* fashionable: not one of them would look ludicrously out of date.

At any given moment today,

there are usually five ways to look ultra up-to-the-minute; ten ways in which to look contemporary; and only about two ways to look really grotesquely out-of-date. Like, say, by wearing a mini-skirt plus platform-soled boots. Even then, you could probably get away with it if you did it with enough conviction.

So you can forget about that expensive old bugbear of looking fashionable and concentrate on wearing clothes you feel happy and look terrific in. Which brings us to Rule Number One of Nouveau Poor dressing:

IT'S NOT SO MUCH WHAT YOU WEAR, IT'S THE WAY YOU THROW IT ALL TOGETHER

You've probably noticed that in the past few years, the fashion looks which have been absolute non-starters have been the old-fashioned Go-Together ones: the suit, or the dress-and-matching-jacket, or the dress-and-matching coat. By the same token, dresses and coats individually haven't been doing frightfully well either. What's come up instead is a look constructed from several elements: skirts or trousers as a basic, combined with sweaters and cardigans, shirts, scarves, jerkins, waistcoats, bits and pieces, with every season producing its own characteristic combinations. Fashion, in a word, is bitty: which is lovely news for us Nouveau Poors.

Take, for instance, that well-cut, fully-lined navy gaberdine skirt you may well have in your wardrobe. Over the past few seasons you might have worn it.

a) With a white Cricket Look V-necked sweater with navy and claret stripes, matching scarf, claret shirt, navy tights and shoes (for spring).

b) With a plain cream shirt, navy tank top, pretty printed silk scarf (informal evening).

c) With a white cotton jacket, navy and white checked shirt, bare tanned legs, navy sandals (summer).

d) With a thick hooded cream cardigan, red flannel shirt, red knitted stockings, navy shoes (autumn).

e) With a plunge-cut white silk shirt, lots of pearls, sheer navy tights and sandals (another informal evening look).

f) With a fur jacket, white beret, navy cashmere classic sweater worn over a white shirt, boots (winter).

See what we mean? Six completely different looks, some classic, some contemporary, all of them equally valid, all built up on one good basic skirt. Note that word good.

Talking about fashion, how does the Nouveau Poor lady work out which looks to back? One answer is by following the fashion pages of newspapers: when they're good, they're the best possible guide to instant fashion news. Pick your favourite and stick to her. From time to time, too, try to see *Elle*, the amazing French women's weekly, and still the best fashion magazine there is. At the start of each season — around September and April — they usually have a couple of fat issues which sum u all the season's newest, excit looks, colours, ways of puttin all together. Any good hairdresser gets in *Elle* for his customers to look at (if yours doesn't, maybe it's time you changed anyway...). If, though, you do have to shell out fifty pence for a copy — you'll find it unbeatable as an authoritative, spirited and inspiring guide to getting chic.

British *Vogue* will show you the best of British design, as well as those French and Italian goodies; *Over 21* is more down-to-earth and practical; *19* and *Honey* are mainly for teenagers. A spot of window-shopping at places like Browns, Wallis, Feathers or the priciest of the local stores and boutiques, can zizz up your ideas a lot, too.

There's usually a strong prevailing colour story every autumn, another in the spring. When it was all tomato or pine green a girl would have felt a bit out of it without at least a touch of these lovely autumnal colours in her wardrobe. And then there was the time when we all suddenly wanted some hot strong Jap colour — shocking pink, jade green or bright yellow, to wear with our blacks. But the colour of the moment can be a pain in the neck too, if everybody takes it up: like that fearsome recent summer when every shop suddenly filled up with sage green, salmon pink and cream. If a colour does nothing for you, ignore it.

Having worked out, at the start of each season, a rough idea of how you want to dress and what colours might be exciting for you, begin by studying what you already own.

This is an essential habit to get into, and brings us to Rule Number Two of Nouveau Poor dressing.

IF YOU CAN'T WEAR IT, FILE IT

Do your filing twice a year, at the end of the summer and at the end of winter. This is a messy, time-consuming chore which will flood your entire bedroom ankle-deep in clothes, scarves, itty-bitty numbers you forgot you owned and terrible old shoes. Do it when you've just had a haircut and your morale is reasonably

high. Do it behind locked doors, with a full-length mirror handy, and a stiff drink too, if necessary. Keep out husbands, lovers, and those worst-of-all counsellors, girl-friends. Don't even contemplate doing it if there are small children around.

Left in peace, with your entire

wardrobe down to the last hat-pin within your view, plan. Eliminate. Co-ordinate. File.

What to eliminate

Clothes you never felt happy in for a single moment, but didn't like to chuck because they were pricey.

The evening dress your husband said made you look pregnant — you'll never be happy in it again unless you are.

Anything that was a quick, cheap version of some passing fashion, and now merely looks cheap.

Any clothes you simply haven't looked at for at least three years.

That dress you wore when you were twenty-two and are going to be slim enough to wear again one of these days. Are you?

Sling them all into a big carrier bag, to be sold off, and wade in once more.

Ennui at once descends. You are now looking at the clothes you found so exciting a year ago, wore all summer or winter, then couldn't wait to pack away. Now here they are again.

The time has come for a spot of FILING. In other words, for putting lovingly back into store a lot of good stuff which is going to have a nice long rest...

Filing

File anything in a colour you're sick to death of because you wore so much of it a year ago — like that good basic tomato.

File, next, the looks that were absolutely of-the-minute at any time within the past six months. The only fashion which dates is the last one, so if you succumbed to some passing fancy like the Chinese Quilted Look, the Cricket Look, or the Khaki Look, file it firmly away for at least six months, because it's just going to shout Last Season's Thing to anybody who looks at it. The fashion before the last, on the other hand, is fine, and everybody will have forgotten it already, so you can safely dig it out again.

File, finally, any clothes you like but are basically a bit bored with: you can both use the rest.

Clothes should be filed clean. Most launderettes have a dry-cleaning section these days and you can take a great big bundle and have it all cleaned in one fell swoop for a fraction of the cost of getting it all cleaned separately. Give it plenty of fresh-airing on hangers afterwards, though, and store it hanging, if possible. If not, store it folded between layers and layers of tissue-paper in a big labelled box.

What you're left looking at now are the clothes you're going to wear this season. Try and see them with a completely fresh eye. Try them on in different combinations. And do bear in mind our Rule Number Three:

NEVER MAKE A MAJOR ALTERATION TO A GOOD GARMENT

That pricey black velvet midi-skirt you bought three years ago: you're sorely tempted to lop a foot off the hem, and give yourself a useful normal-length black skirt. You won't, though. What you'll do is wreck the line and proportions of what was once a good garment, and end up with a curiously unconvincing skirt. And who says you can't wear a midi-skirt this winter anyway? With boots, a spot of fur, and lots of pearls, it could be a super-glamorous Anna Karenina look for a winter party. We know one fashion editor, at that, who wore the same Rive Gauche wrap-around black wool midi-skirt for five winters running without altering it an inch.

The pale pink suede waistcoat that you bought in a moment of extravagance years back, occasionally wear with jeans, and forget about most of the time: try it with your narrow black skirt, and a very pale pink shirt — you could dye a white cotton one — and one of those Indian scarves that go for a song these days in very hot pink plus.

The black velvet blazer you wore to death two winters ago with black trousers? And which is looking past its best? Keep it for Slumchic weekend wear: with jeans, an old shirt, a big brassy belt. Just buy one thing to go with it: a black, blue and white tartan scarf from the boys' department of a big store.

And how about that collarless brown silk shirt that cost a fortune but hardly ever gets worn because you don't look terribly good in a collarless shirt? It becomes an overshirt, of course: on top of a pale cream shirt, tucked into your best black skirt, for a dressier, more formal version of the shirt-and-skirt look.

And that red wool flannel shirt? Make it work like a jacket. Wear it belted on top of a thick white rollneck sweater, with a skirt, or wear it open, unbelted, over thick sweater and trousers.

The lissom little black jersey dinner dress you've worn for after-eight so often you can hardly stand the sight of it? Turn it into daytime wear, of course: put it over a thin white rollneck sweater, put a big sporty belt round the waist, add a touch of massive, sporty jewellery, boots, and there you are. Clothes can quite often be given a whole new lease of life when you stop thinking of them as exclusively for day or evening wear.

At the end of all this swopping and teaming and trying on, you should have come up with four or five completely new and up-to-the-minute looks.

AND SOME OBVIOUS GAPS
Gap number one:
If it's autumn — is usually the cover-up. Having got your skirts and tops and bits and pieces together, what do you put on top that's going to look smashing and keep you warm in the depths of winter? The answer doesn't have to be a coat. It could be a jacket — fur or otherwise. Or a cape. Or a hugely thick cardigan with extra layers of scarf for when it freezes. Or a raincoat.

But the first question to ask yourself is — must you have it right now? Because in most of Britain, the weather seldom gets absolutely arctic much before Christmas. And bang after Christmas come the January sales when shops lop ten per cent, twenty per cent, thirty per cent or even more off perfectly good clothes with reckless abandon. The fur jacket or the good classic trench-coat you'll wear for ever, the thick cardigan or the useful cape: they'll all be around in early January waiting for you. Greatly reduced. Just when it turns really chilly. So what's the hurry?

You'll notice, by the way, that we said fur jacket rather than fur coat. There was a reason, and it's this. Invest money in a full-length mink coat, and your investment goes sour on you the minute there's a noticeable change in skirt length. Two or three inches one way or the other can make you look a real dowd — and who needs £1000s worth of mink to help them feel dowdy?

Gap number two is Shoes

Nothing switches on that current look faster than the right, contemporary shoes; nothing destroys the whole effect faster than drab, boring out-of-date shoes. But do you have to go to the really pricey shops and shell out £19.99 minimum to get that spot-on pair? Not any more. It would be nice, of course, to be shod only in the finest, softest of glove leathers crafted by clever Italians. But nobody is going to look very closely at your shoes once they've taken in the general effect. And you may be astonished to find what amazingly good value you can find at stores like Freeman, Hardy & Willis, Bata or Dolcis, if your eyes are sharp enough. Littlewoods have some of the best ultra-cheap chain-store shoes, though they're seldom made of real leather. And if you get to a main branch of Marks & Spencer early enough in the season, you might find the odd example of really startling value and inspiration. Among the medium-priced shops, the Sacha chain have marvellously chic shoes, but alas, their favourite last is too narrow for most of the girls we know...

How about boots? We ourselves now tend simply to collect boots — baggy or close-fitting — the way we collect scarves or belts or good skirts. And it's amazing how the oldest, most rotten down-at-heel boots go on looking quite good given even a minimum of polish and expert cobbling. Meanwhile, of course, they're saving the wear and tear on your current best new boots, if you could swing a pair this season. But boots and shoes, like cover-ups, are another buy it's crazy to make at the start of the season unless you're desperate; last winter's January sales were stuffed with boot and shoe bargains, often down to half-price; including one amazing Made-in-Italy pair of baggy boots, in black or that costly-looking lacquer red, going for a song plus a fiver at Freeman, Hardy & Willis. Admittedly they were not real leather, but for a fiver, who cares?

Talking about sales, may we slip in yet another Nouveau Poor Rule here?

NEVER BUY ANYTHING IN A SALE UNLESS YOU KNOW YOU NEED IT NOW
Buying stuff that *might* come in, some day, just because it's half-normal price, is one sure way to load your wardrobe with expensive junk.

BASIC GOOD BUYS
The key garment: The basic buy of the season is your real Basic,

and according to current fashion, it may be a skirt or a pair of trousers. Either way, this one garment is going to be the key to a whole season's changed look. Think of the midi-skirt, and the swirling Jap-inspired peasant midi-skirt, and that exciting narrow look that made bulky sweaters beautiful again; and you'll realise at once how vital it is to get this particular basic right if you want to look contemporary. And it's a drag not to have the makings of at least one new current fashion outfit.

Scarves: You'll certainly need to buy at least one new scarf, whether it's a schoolboy muffler, a peasanty fringed wool square, or a Woolworth's silver-checked gauze. There's always an important scarf in any fashion look — like those striped Missoni ones which finally got knocked off by everyone. And one twenty-five franc French chain-store muffler in stinging pink can give a touch of Jap to an entire wardrobe.

Well-cut skirts: cheap or otherwise — in silk or cotton. You can always dye them bright red if you get bored with them, but we don't think it's possible to have too many good skirts.

The current T-shirt: there's always a season's T-shirt shape. Buy it in your favourite colour and never, ever throw it away. One girl we know reckons she could put on an illustrated history of T-shirts any time; Biba 1971, was, she claims, a particularly vintage year.

Anything well-cut in blue denim: need we say more?

Amusing bits of costume jewellery: bug pins, Bill Gibb bees, British Museum reproduction pieces (terrific value, these), cheap coloured bangles; you can sometimes pull a whole look together with just the right dotty or effectively placed piece.

Good-quality belts in real leather: they'll last you for ever.

Well-designed sweaters: preferably without a pattern unless it's something absolutely classic like a fairisle decoration or stripes.

None of these Good Buys, incidentally should ever find their way into your chuck-out bag when you file, however temporarily bored with them you may be.

BAD BUYS

This season's shape in an ultra-cheap version: it will give you no great joy this season — and you can burn it thereafter.

Cheap, unlined skirts: the only good buy in skirts is a well-made one, lined, in a good fabric. Anything else is an expensive waste of time.

The Very Newest Thing: it's the look all the fashion editors are suddenly on about. Oh, the fun of wearing it the week it's all over Miss Selfridge...and oh, the desperate gloom of it a month later. Example: that funny shaded look.

Any up-to-the-minute fashion you're not certain you'll be able to manage: we never did discover just what you were supposed to do with a shawl, for instance.

Cheap evening dresses bought in a rush for a special occasion: they'll look it, you'll feel it. How about wearing your old long skirt, a startling new top, and a brand-new make-up instead?

WHERE TO GET IT

Having worked out what you need, where are you going to get it? There are lots of women around who still only know about fashion shops. Here are some of the alternatives...

Make it yourself

We ourselves can't — both of us are hopeless with a pattern — so we can only admire and envy the clever ladies who can run themselves up a ravishing summer skirt with its own matching scarf out of a couple of yards of printed cotton. Turn an old blanket into a jolly winter cape. Add amusing patches to old worn-out sweater elbows. Make their own cheap towelling bathrobes instead of having to covet the hopelessly overpriced ones you see in shops. Lucky them.

As a special bonus, we asked Mary Quant to design them a real Nouveau Poor Basic. Here is her stunning answer: a go-over-almost-anything tabard, cut with typical Quant dash and economy, and designed to pull two halves of an outfit wittily and stylishly together. Pick a firmish fabric: make it in a vivid patterned jersey, like the one Mary chose, or a clear bright red wool, or a warm black mohair. Wear it over a big-sleeved blouse and long black skirt for extra warmth; over sweater and trousers — with a big wide belt around it — for extra warmth; over a plain contrasting dress, sashed with a colourful cummerbund, for fun. You'll need up to two metres of fabric — and no more than a spare evening. You'll end up with a Quant Original. The tabard is made of two identical pieces — one for the back, the other for the front: the two belt-pieces button one over the other, round back or front as the mood takes you. Careful perfectionist binding round the edges give our Quant tabard its special chic.

To make the pattern:

Start by buying a huge sheet of squared-off paper. Cut out a big rectangle measuring $43\frac{1}{2}''$ by $20''$. Fold it in two lengthways. Then place folded edge towards you and measure out the pattern as follows:

Along right hand edge, measure and mark points from fold as follows: $2\frac{5}{8}''$ — point A

$6\frac{1}{2}''$ — point B

From B measure in $1\frac{1}{8}''$ on a line parallel with fold. Mark this C. Join A and C with a straight line.

Along fold measure $11\frac{3}{4}''$ from right hand edge, mark this D. Join A to D with a faint line.

Along A/D measure $6''$, and mark E. From E measure $\frac{3}{8}''$ in on a line parallel with righthand edge. Mark F. Along D/E measure half way, and mark a point $\frac{1}{4}''$ in, parallel with righthand edge, mark this G. Repeat this along E/A and mark this H.

Connect D, G, F, H and A with a smooth curve. *This forms the low neckline.*

From the far right hand corner measure $14\frac{1}{4}''$ along the far edge and mark this J. Measure in $1\frac{7}{8}''$ to a point on a line parallel with right hand edge, and mark this K.

Join K to C with a faint line. This should measure $13\frac{1}{4}''$. Half way along this line ($6\frac{5}{8}''$) measure in $\frac{7}{8}''$ on a line parallel with the right hand edge. Mark this L.

Connect K, L, C with a smooth curve. This is the deep armhole line.

Along the left hand edge (the hem) measure in $9\frac{1}{4}''$ from the fold and mark this M.

Connect M to K with a straight line. 2″ along this line from K mark point N. A two inch half belt will be inserted from K to N on the front.

The pattern is now ready to cut out.

Cut along M, K, L, C, A, H, F, G and D. Open out and this will serve as both front and back patterns and has $\frac{1}{2}''$ turning allowed for all round except shoulders which are $\frac{3}{4}''$.

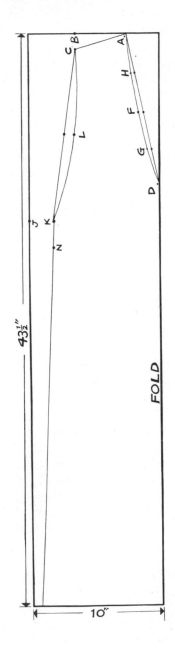

HOW TO LAY OUT YOUR PATTERN
42"/54" (107cm./137cm.) = 2 YARDS (OR 2 METRES)

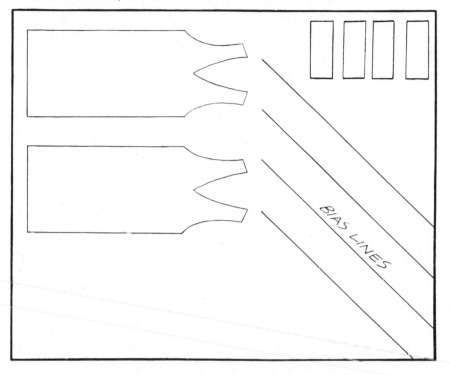

58"/68"(147 cm./172 cm.) = 1·50 YARDS (OR 1·50 METRES)

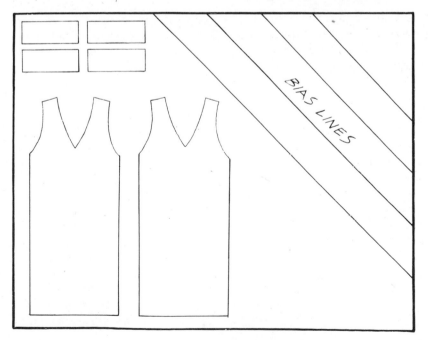

To make up the Tabard

Cutting: You'll need two yards of 42"-54" fabric, or one and a half if the fabric is more than 58" wide.

When you have made your paper pattern, place it on the fabric according to the diagram and make sure that the centre of the garment from top to bottom is on the straight grain of the fabric. Cut two of the shapes.

On the straight grain of the fabric, cut four rectangles 16" by 3" for the two half belts. Cut to a point at one end if you wish.

For the binding, measure along the raw edges of the sides and hem, double this measurement, and add a few inches for the joins. Measure the neck edge, add at least 8", plus any extra for joins. Measure the edges of the belt to be bound (you do not need to bind the short edge which is attached to the tabard) and add a bit for joins if necessary.

It is best to cut the binding strips on the bias of the fabric, as shown in the cutting diagram, although on firm jerseys like the striped acrylic Mary used for her tabard the straight grain can be used, and this gives the pretty contrasting effect shown in the photograph. Cut the binding in $1\frac{1}{2}$" wide strips from the remaining fabric (the finished binding will measure $\frac{3}{4}$") until you have sufficient.

Sewing: Now sew the two main tabard pieces together at the shoulders, with right sides together, stitching $\frac{3}{4}$" from the edge. Press seams open and flat.

Join some of the binding strips together so that you have one continuous piece long enough to go round the sides and hem of the tabard. Place the right side of the binding to the wrong side of the tabard. Tack firmly before you sew and be careful not to stretch the binding when tacking it to the garment. Clip in to the seam line on the seam allowance of the binding at the corners. Stitch, pivoting at corners. Press the seam open and flat, trimming away all the fullness on the seam allowance at corners. Fold the entire bias strip across onto the right side of the garment, easing under the fullness at the corners to make a neat diagonal edge. Press. Then turn under $\frac{1}{4}$" along the raw edge of the binding, tack and press. Either machine stitch close to fold, or slipstitch. Finally, slipstitch the edges of the binding together at the corners.

To bind the neck edges you will need two strips, each a good 4" longer than the raw edges. Place the right side of the facing against the wrong side of the tabard, raw edges together, and stitch $\frac{1}{2}$" from the edge to a point directly beneath the central V, leaving the extra binding free. The stitching on each piece will meet at this point: be careful not to catch up the other piece of binding when you are attaching the second strip. Now fold the tabard down the centre front (and back), right sides together, pin the loose binding strips together on top, and stitch vertically downwards, from the V to the edge, as close to the fold of the tabard as possible. Open out the seams, clip the neck edge of the tabard in to the seamline at the V, and press the seams carefully open and flat. Trim away any superfluous fabric in the seam allowance. Now fold the entire facing through to the right side of the tabard, and press across. Fold under $\frac{1}{4}''$ on the raw edge (you will need to trim the point away slightly), tack, press and machine or slipstitch in place.

To make the belts, first prepare two open ended lengths of binding. For each belt, take two of the rectangles and place them right sides together sandwiching the binding in between so that the three raw edges lie together. Tack, clipping the seam allowance of the binding at corners, as above. Stitch. Open out, press binding across, fold under $\frac{1}{4}''$, press and stitch, finishing off the corners as described above. The end which will be attached to the tabard will be raw and unbound. Turn the edges in on themselves and oversew. Slipstitch the belts very firmly behind the binding on the tabard, where indicated on the pattern.

Make a buttonhole on one, and sew a button on the other, according to how loose you would like it to be.

Knit it yourself

Any woman who knows one end of a knitting needle from the other is laughing up her hand-knitted sleeves these days. The priciest knitwear in the shops is cunningly designed to look as though Granny ran it up for you; the stitches that look chic-est and most up to the minute are common or garden old stocking or garter stitch; the shapes couldn't be simpler.

Here's our own Nouveau Poor Basic — a neo-classic with a minimum of fussy detail. We had it knitted up in bold stripes of loganberry and white: a lovely spring or summer holiday look, to be worn with jeans or shorts, or just a plain cotton skirt. It's fairly long, in keeping with the current feeling for a lot of sweater, but if you want to lop a couple of inches or so off the length, the instructions tell you how. And from the same instructions you can also knit it up plain, in any good solid colour that slots into your autumn and winter wardrobe.

It's made in Paton's Purple Heather 4-ply, a firm springy yarn that's sixty per cent wool and forty per cent acrylic. And it's machine-washable. There are nearly forty colours to choose from, including all the obvious basics like black, white, navy. And unless prices have shot up since we went to press, it should cost you well under four pounds.

MATERIALS: Of Patons Purple Heather 4 ply, *Plain Version:* 15 [16, 17, 17] (25 gram) balls, *Striped Version:* 8 [8, 9, 9](25 gram) balls Main Shade and 7 [8, 8, 9] (25 gram) balls of Contrast.

Pair each Nos $2\frac{3}{4}$mm and $3\frac{1}{4}$mm needles. Needle sizes quoted are Metric. Equivalent UK sizes are No 12 for $2\frac{3}{4}$mm and No 10 for $3\frac{1}{4}$mm.

It is essential to work to the stated tension, and Patons & Baldwins Limited cannot accept responsibility for the finished product if any yarn other than the recommended Patons yarn is used.

MEASUREMENTS: To fit 32 [34, 36, 38] in (81 [86, 91, 97] cm) bust; length from top of shoulders 25 [25½, 26, 26½] in (63 [65, 66, 67] cm); sleeve seam, 18½ [19, 19, 19] in (47 [48, 48, 48] cm).

SIZES: The figures in square brackets [ ] refer to the 3 larger sizes.

TENSION: 14 sts and 18 rows to 2 in measured over stocking stitch on No 3¼mm needles.

ABBREVIATIONS: K = knit; P = purl; st = stitch; inc = increase by working into front and back of stitch; dec = decrease by working 2 stitches together; beg = beginning; alt = alternate; patt = pattern; in = inches; cm = centimetres; mm = millimetres; MS = Main Shade; C = Contrast; M1 = make 1 stitch by picking up horizontal loop lying before next stitch and working into back of it.

PLAIN VERSION

BACK: With No 2¾mm needles, cast on 116 [122, 130, 136] sts. ** Work 1½ in K1, P1 rib. *Next row* — Rib 12 [13, 13, 14], M1, (rib 23 [24, 26, 27] M1) 4 times, rib 12 [13, 13, 14] (121 [127, 135, 141] sts). **

Change to No 3¼mm needles and starting with a K row, work straight in stocking stitch until Back measures 16½ in, ending with a P row.

***Place a marker at each end of last row.

Continue straight until Back measures 24 [24½, 25, 25½] in, ending with a P row.

Shape shoulders by casting off 2 sts at beg of next 6 [6, 4, 4] rows, 5 sts at beg of following 6 [6, 8, 8] rows, 8 [9, 9, 10] sts at beg of following 4 rows.

Leave remaining 47 [49, 51, 53] sts on a length of yarn.

FRONT: Work as for Back until 12 [12, 14, 14] rows less have been worked before start of shoulder shaping, thus ending with right side facing for next row.

**Divide for neck* as follows:- *Next row* — K 46 [48, 52, 54] sts, turn and leave remaining sts on a spare needle.

Keeping side edge straight, dec 1 st at neck edge on every row until 37 [39, 42, 44] sts remain. Work 2 [2, 3, 3] rows straight, thus ending with a P row.

Shape shoulder by casting off 2 sts at beg of next and following 2 [2, 1, 1] alt rows, 5 sts at beg of following 3 [3, 4, 4] alt rows, 8 [9, 9, 10] sts at beg of following alt row.

Work 1 row straight. Cast off remaining 8 [9, 9, 10] sts.

With right side facing, leave centre 29 [31, 31, 33] sts on a length of yarn, rejoin yarn to remaining sts, K to end.

Complete to correspond with first side, reversing shapings.

SLEEVES: With No 2¾mm needles, cast on 52 [54, 56, 58] sts. **Work 1½ in K1, P1 rib. *Next row* — Rib 2 [3, 1, 2], M1, (rib 3, M1) 16 [16, 18, 18] times, rib 2 [3, 1, 2] (69 [71, 75, 77] sts)**

Change to No 3¼mm needles and starting with a K row, work in stocking stitch, shaping sides by inc 1 st at each end of next [5th, 9th,

next] and every following 8th [7th, 6th, 6th] row until there are 107 [113, 121, 127] sts.

***Work straight until sleeve seam measures 18½ [19, 19, 19] in, ending with a P row. Cast off.

MAKE UP AND NECKBAND: Omitting ribbing, press lightly following instructions on the ball band.

Join right shoulder seam.

With right side facing and No. 2¾mm needles, *knit up* 33 [35, 37, 39] sts down left side of neck, K across 29 [31, 31, 33] sts at centre, *knit up* 33 [35, 37, 39] sts up right side of neck, K across 47 [49, 51, 53] sts from Back (142 [150, 156, 164] sts).

Work 10 rows K 1, P 1 rib. Cast off evenly in rib.

Join left shoulder seam and Neckband. Join sleeve seams and side seams to markers. Insert Sleeves. Press seams.

STRIPED VERSION

NOTE: Join in and break off colours as required.

BACK: With No. 2¾mm needles and MS, cast on 116 [122, 130, 136] sts and work as for Plain Version from ** to **.

Change to No 3¼mm needles, join in C and starting with a K row, work in stocking stitch and patt of 14 rows C, 14 rows MS until Back measures 16½ in, ending with a P row.

Keeping continuity of stripe patt, complete as for Back of Plain Version from *** to end.

FRONT: Work as for Back until 12 [12, 14, 14] rows less have been worked before start of shoulder shaping, thus ending with right side facing for next row.

Keeping continuity of stripe patt, work as for Front of Plain Version from ** to end.

SLEEVES: With No. 2¾mm needles and MS, cast on 52 [54, 56, 58] sts and work in rib as for Sleeves of Plain Version from ** to **.

Change to No.3¼ mm needles, join in C and start with a K row, work in stocking stitch and stripe patt of 14 rows C, 14 rows MS, shaping sides as for Plain Version until there are 107 [113, 121, 127] sts.

Complete as for Sleeves of Plain Version from *** to end.

MAKE UP AND NECKBAND: Make Up as for Plain Version, working Neckband in M.S.

Second-hand clothes shops

(You'll find them pompously disguised as Dress Agencies in your local Yellow Pages.) A second-hand clothes shop is the most off-putting sight in the world. Don't be put off. Grit your teeth, wade in, and remember that if your own entire wardrobe were thrown on to one rail, it would look just as tatty and unappetising. You'll find amazingly good stuff, slung out by the capricious rich who can *still* afford to buy whole new wardrobes at Browns every season, and are too mean to give it all away; you'll find eighteen pound sweaters, hardly worn, going for three pounds; you'll find, perhaps, a Jean Muir or a John Bates hanging unloved and waiting for you and your seven pounds fifty. Remember that some of the world's greatest clothes have absolutely no hanger-appeal.

Jumble Sales

Consult your local newspaper and use your eyes on local notice-boards to track these down. GET THERE EARLY — there are experts in the field. Once inside all the above applies, only ten times more so. At a tenth of the price. Remember you can always have your purchases cleaned.

Sitting-room and garage sales

Newest invention of our inflated times, these are rather more private affairs — nothing to stop you organising your own, with the help of several dependable friends. At best, you'll pick up a couple of useful low-cost additions to your wardrobe. At worst you'll get rid of your own mistakes for a price.

Antique clothes stalls

Personally, we're a bit bored with that old 'thirties print crepe dress bit. But other goodies you might find here are beautiful antique lace blouses — smashing with jeans — fur jackets or scarves at knockdown prices — or intriguingly dated sweaters.

Auctions

Worth keeping an eye on your local auction rooms: all kinds of unlikely merchandise seems to be cropping up there these days, as well as the more usual paintings and antiques. Phillips Son & Neale in London, for instance, are famous for their fur auctions, at which you can sometimes pick up a snip of a fox fur jacket: you can go along beforehand and get a good look at the stuff, too.

Special offers in the fashion pages of magazines and newspapers

These are almost always true value. The fashion editor has spotted a gap, persuaded some friendly manufacturer into producing a special, and is offering it at his price plus, probably, a token amount to cover the publication's expenses, instead of a shop's normal hundred per cent mark-up. For instance, *Cosmopolitan* had an amazing nightdress for £5.50 that would have cost at least £12.00 in a shop; *Over-21* a stylish silk shirt for £6.99 at a time when similar shirts were selling for £15 in the shops.

Markets

Theoretically a splendid new source for Nouveau Poor clothes. In fact, beware. They can afford not to add on the normal shop mark-up of a hundred per cent to branded clothes — but lots of stallholders do, all the same. We happily bought a quilted waistcoat a year ago in one London market — only to find it was fifty pence cheaper in Miss Selfridge. As for all that ethnic cheesecloth — it needs to be well-made these days to look something.

Children's ranges

Another big plus in being

small-sized is that you can raid children's wear departments in shops and chain-stores. Marks & Spencer, for instance, were running a lovely white and navy checked cotton shirt for school-children recently for a really cheap price and their basic drip-dry white cotton shirts are always value.

Army surplus shops

Duffel coats or Merchant Navy sweaters, fatigues and khaki overalls, drill dungarees and flannel shirts — a whole range of brisk, stolen-from-the-chaps stuff to be cleverly (very cleverly, please) teamed with well-cut trousers, gold belts, snappy sweaters or pretty shirts — and the right boots.

Working clothes

Overalls and boiler suits, nurses' uniforms and surgical gowns, white cotton waiters' jackets and red painters' smocks: most of them made of cotton too, the easiest fabric in the world to dye.

There's no end to the possibilities. As long as (we're sorry to keep harping on this) you're that nice neat size ten or twelve.

DO YOU SPOIL YOUR CLOTHES?

Having picked, co-ordinated and filed your wardrobe, it makes Nouveau Poor sense to be good to it. And we don't mean spending enormous sums of money on cleaners' bills. On the contrary. Lady Rendlesham, formidably chic directrice of all the St Laurent Rive Gauche shops in Britain, thinks that clothes shouldn't go too often to the cleaners: "It wears them out faster. It's much better for your clothes if you learn to look after them yourself. Teach yourself to spot-clean well,* and you won't have to send everything off to be cleaned. Get into the habit, too, of giving them a good brush and a gentle shake from time to time before you put them away. And teach yourself to press them properly: pressing is a great art. Englishwomen never seem to have learned the art of looking after their clothes properly — something most Continental women are carefully taught by their mothers. But it's a skill that has to be learned and practised just like cooking; and like cooking, anyone can do it well if they want to."

*About that spot-cleaning, though. Even the most encouraging of the do-it-yourself manuals get a bit daunting and technical on the subject of do-it-yourself dry-cleaning. So unless you're pretty sure of yourself, don't ruin your one and only Jean Muir for ever, attempting to spot-clean away that dab of French dressing on the bodice...

Face-Saving

FACE-SAVING

"There are four fundamental cosmetics...which don't come out of jars and bottles...they are un-restricted, available to every-body: sleep, diet, exercise, rest for twenty minutes a day after lunch..."

That was British *Vogue* in 1942, putting a bravely patriotic face on the distressing war-time dearth of vital skin-stuffs.

But it doesn't have to be war-time for the advice to be sound. As far as your skin is concerned, the best things in life are free, and anything those pricey little pots can do for it come a long way behind.

FIRST THE BAD NEWS

A couple of the very best things you can do for your skin will actually save you money: cut down on or cut out smoking and drinking. Heavy smoking is death to a clear vital-looking skin and bright eyes. And even amateurs can spot the heavy habitual drinkers at a glance, from their blotched and patchy skins, and those tell-tale puffy bits round the never-quite-clear eyes. One of the reasons, inciden-tally, why lots of alcohol is bad for your skin is because it's fear-fully acid — wine even more so than spirits: which is why beauty wizards like Countess Csaky are always on at their clients to drink a spoonful of fresh lemon juice in hot water first thing every morning — very antacid — and to drink lashings of water generally.

There are two other arch-enemies of skin that it will cost you precisely nothing to avoid, although it could cost you plenty to try and repair the damage they do. One is too much sun and the other is too much make-up.

Long term or short term, too much sun is terrible news for skins, and drying it up is only one of the deadly things it does. If you're holidaying somewhere where the sun is really fierce, don't ever go out in it unless you're wearing a big beautiful shady straw hat. You'll still get a strong dose of sunshine anyway, since sun is bounced back up into your face from sand, from pavements, from cafe-tables, even. So if you want to be ultra-careful, use a filter cream on your face all the time. Almost any suntan cream that claims to act as a screen or filter will do: the great thing is to use enough of it, and to pick one that your skin gets along with — not much point picking on some pricey stuff which you think perfect, if you can only afford one tiny tube of it.

If everybody around you is competing obsessively for the deepest tan, and you feel drearily pale and out of it, put on a tanned face out of a bottle: even the sharpest eyes can't always detect that Guerlain's Teint Dore isn't for real.

As for too much make-up: Countess Csaky, world-famous skin-expert has violent views: "Nothing is worse for skin than all that terrible brown stuff that people put on their faces — cement and oil, it doesn't give the poor skin a chance to breathe. I notice that young people today are much more sensible: plenty of eye make-up and a nice deep lipstick, but no make-up at all on their faces quite often...just the lightest of creams, very lightly powdered over...very sensible..."

CLEANSING

If beauty experts are unan-imous about how lousy sun is for your skin, they're equally voci-ferous about the need to get it really CLEAN. Nothing is worse for it than old grease and make-up and atmospheric dirt clogging up the pores. And just one swipe is seldom enough to get off all the gunge that accumulates on a city face in the course of a day: keep going till your skin is really clean.

Which means, obviously, that you're going to get through a fair amount of whichever cleanser you use. Does it have to be a "good" one? We put the question to Joan Price, one-time beauty editor who now gives impartial advice on skin-care and make-up across most cosmetic ranges to clients at her Face Places. Joan is brisk about the pricey ones. "I'd never waste money on sophisti-cated cleaners and toners: they're much of a muchness in any range. The up-market ranges tend to spend more money on their older-lady creams — and at Estee Lauder and Ultima II prices you're into the older-lady market — so their cleaners will be very nice to use. But you will be paying for packaging and presen-tation. On the other hand, some of the cheaper creams and milks tend to be a bit fierce: a certain price-range attracts a particular age-group and they tailor the product accordingly. Lemon Delph and Anne French, for in-stance, and the cleansers in most of the cheaper ranges are aimed at resilient — and often oily — teenage skins: they may be a bit tough on over thirty faces. It's basically a question of finding a cleanser that your skin is obviously happy with — and then using it properly."

Joan Price — practising what she preaches — has produced her own brand of no-nonsense unscented cleanser in a plastic bottle. Other economic buys you can experiment with are Astral, Crowe's Cremine, Boots Cold Cream, Leichner's Theatrical Make-Up Remover, Johnson's Baby Lotion — but for dry skins only — and Max Factor's Cleansing Cold Cream, one of their best-ever and most successful products.

Soap and water? "Only if you use softened water and a plain scentless complexion soap or washing cream: it's the scent and the binding agent in soaps that are drying because they're alkaline, and a healthy skin has a slightly acid mantle of natural oil or sebum. Even then, soap and water can only wash your skin: they can't possibly get off make-up because it always contains oils that aren't soluble in water."

At present-day paper prices, the extravagent way to remove your cleanser is with fistfuls of paper tissues. Instead, clean off creams with plain towelling facecloths, moistened with tepid water, but don't ever use one more than once. If you could see the germs breeding on that dirty cloth, you would be quite ill, so do boil them with soft soap.

More simply, use cotton wool moistened with tepid water. And you won't, of course, be wasting money on those charming packets of rainbow-coloured cotton wool balls. Boots' enormous rolls of Surgical Cotton Wool with

Rayon work out just about ten times cheaper (cost the price out per gramme, like washing-up powder) and are just as effective.

As well as regular daily cleansing, your skin needs a deep down thorough pore-cleansing from time to time. And one of the best ways to do it is to give it a mini-sauna. Leslie Kenton, beauty editor of *Harpers & Queen* with the clear soft skin of a child, does so regularly herself and strongly recommends it. "Once a week — and more often if your skin is really greasy — wrap a Turkish towel around your head and steam your face over a bowl of very hot water for about five to eight minutes. Throw some herbs into the water — either dried from a health shop, or fresh from your garden. The vapours released from the herbs help cleanse the skin once the pores are open. Different herbs do different things: mint, for instance is very stimulating to the skin; rosemary is soothing."

"Personally I use dried herbs specially blended for a Facial Steam Bath by Annemarie Borlind." You can buy a pack containing enough for about twenty-five saunas from the London

Health Centre for about £2.25.

This kind of steaming deep-cleanses pores and leaves them wide open afterwards. Close them with a gentle splash of tepid water or tonic. We don't need to add that you should be very careful not to scald your skin. And forget about steaming if you have an exceptionally fragile skin or thread veins.

Another way to give your skin a good deep-down clean-up is by putting on a face-mask after you've removed your make-up. But it doesn't have to be a pricey bought one: plain Fullers Earth from a chemist, mixed with enough water to turn it into a smooth mud, will bring off a lot of the surface debris. Add a dash of lemon juice to make it even more bracing. Almost anything in your kitchen will do something to your face if plastered or smoothed on and left, and beauty pages of magazines are full of do-it-yourself recipes for face-masks. Or you could try a couple of those suggested in two do-it-yourself beauty books. Donna Lawson, in *Mother Nature's Beauty Cupboard* (Robert Hale & Company, London 1973), suggests a honey and lemon mask for normal skins: a tablespoon of slightly warmed honey combined with a teaspoon of lemon juice, blended, applied to your face, and left on for half an hour. Very moisturising, she claims.

And Dian Dincin Buchman, in *Feed Your Face,* (Duckworth, London, 1973), recommends Brewer's Yeast as a facial for ladies with oily skins. Stir the powder into a stiff paste with milk, or yogurt, or rose-water,

pat on to a clean face, wash off with tepid water and finish by closing your pores with a chilly astringent.

Face-masks are never the big best-sellers in any cosmetic range, and cosmetic houses tend to throw in a little mumbo-jumbo to help boost their sales-appeal. Wear them lying down, they suggest, relaxed after a warm bath, in a darkened room, with eye-pads soaked in witch-hazel over your peacefully-closed eyes. You can forget all this time-wasting nonsense and simply put them on before your bath.

TONING

How about toning, then — second of the magical cleanse-tone-nourish trio which beauty experts used to preach?

According to Countess Csaky, the best toner of all comes free from the tap. "Forget about tonics and astringents and all that pretty stuff — it's an absolute waste of money. There's nothing better for your face than a splash of cold water — it's splendid for tightening up pores and firming the skin, and as long as you have a little oil or moisturiser on your face, it can't possibly dry it. If you take off your make-up thoroughly enough with damp cotton-wool, you won't need a tonic anyway."

MOISTURISING

Our faces are the only bits of us that are permanently on show, and they take a terrible beating, poor things. Nothing is right for them, really. Freezing cold and driving rain dry them out; too much sun withers them. They aren't mad about air-conditioning and they don't take kindly to central heating. One way and another, they need constant careful moisturising to combat all this enemy action, and beauty editors are as unanimous now in urging us to Cleanse-Moisturise as they used to be about cleanse-tone-and-nourish.

But once more, it doesn't have to be an expensive moisturiser to be perfectly satisfactory for your skin. If it feels right on your skin, then it's fine for your skin.

One middle-price moisturiser that several beauty editors personally swear by is Oil of Ulay. Innoxa don't have a dud cream in their range, and their moisturiser with Amalene is particularly good. Boots' No. 7 moisturisers (one of them with Vitamin E), Woolworth's own Evette brand and Rimmel are other good bargain buys. The ones you buy in health shops are not only relatively cheap: they tend to be free of the artificial colouring and the cheap mineral oils which can irritate sensitive skin in more commercial cheap ranges.

"I'd be afraid to stop," proclaims the smooth-faced beauty in one ad. for a really expensive skin cream. Personally, we'd be afraid to get started on a long-term course of anything so costly. Cosmetic houses plugging their miracle creams are mostly cashing in on a woman's ingrained conviction that you actually can do miraculous things to your skin from the outside. But as Mary Davis Peters, shrewd and down-to-earth beauty editor of *Over 21* points out, "Really and truly, no skin food is much more than a super-moisturiser performing two functions: lubrication and occlusiveness; in other words, keeping moisture in. Your skin isn't "fed" from the outside; what you eat and drink provides the nutrients that build skin cells, and proper cleaning and moisturising keep it in good shape." (Take a look at your skin when you next have a really vile hangover to work out if this is or isn't true...)

So you needn't feel that you're short-changing your skin if you're sticking to cheaper creams rather than treating it to the facial equivalent of caviar.

You could always try an avocado instead, actually. Next time you eat one, don't throw away the skin: smooth the inside of it all over your clean face just before you step into your evening bath. "Its full of polyunsaturated fats that your skin just laps up," says Leslie Kenton, "and very good for a dry skin". She herself is a vitamin addict; before her evening bath, she creams off her make-up then squeezes the oil from one Vitamin E and one Vitamin A & D capsule over her face and neck, leaving it to soak in gently during her bath, and removing any excess oiliness when she gets out.

If you really feel, though, that you can't bear anything but the best on your skin, don't just rush to the Ritzy end of the cosmetics department in your local store: wait until your favourite firm is having its own elegant version of a sale. In other words, until they're giving away gratis a whole boxful of little goodies from the range to anyone buying a couple of products. That way, you may be shelling out good money for your chosen buy, but at least you'll be getting to try others out for free. Ultima II, Geminesse, Lancome, Clinique and Estee Lauder are among the houses that do this regularly: it's simply a question of watching your local store and biding your time.

And talking about sales, we notice that the cosmetic houses in the middle price-range have recently taken to joining in the real twice-yearly thing. So, if you're a fan of a particular Juvena, Yardley, Max Factor, Helena Rubinstein or Revlon skin-care product, hang on till the July or January sales before re-stocking — with any luck they'll be running a special giant economy size of it at a bargain price.

Incidentally, unless you have cast-iron sales-resistance, its unwise to approach those smiling, friendly ladies in their pretty pastel overalls when you've got lots of money, a cheque book, or a credit-card in your bag. Before you know where you are, they'll have helpfully sold you a complete skin-care programme, with many sympathetic cluckings about the state of your skin, and you'll be thirty pounds down the spout.

Occasionally, we all make a boob and invest in a huge pot of something that our skin at once tells us that it doesn't like. When that happens, abandon it and cut your losses. Use it up as a body-lotion, or give it to a girl-friend — it may suit her a treat. Soldiering on with it isn't just false economy but sheer cruelty to skin.

In addition to these whims, your skin has one other hang-up: it can't stand routine. Go on using the same same old cleanser and moisturiser year in, year out, and no matter how much they once suited your skin, it will go on strike eventually and start acting up. This is one reason why those clever French beauty houses are always bringing out what they call "les Traitements Choc": special creams to be used in short bursts, as a regular change from ordinary creams in their range. You can get much the same effect at much less cost simply by switching brands from time to time.

YOUR BODY

The rest of your body, mercifully, doesn't need anything like the loving care you have to lavish on your face — mainly because it doesn't get the same exposure. And even if you could afford the cash-price of regular head-to-toe moisturising with one of the many new body-lotions on the market, we can't imagine many women who could spare the time and the energy. The best — and the cheapest — way to stop your body skin getting dried up is to steer clear of what dries it up: sun and hard water. Hard water dries up skin like mad: if your local tap water is hard, don't get in a bath until you've thrown in a tablespoonful of borax — buy it by the kilo from Boots — it will make the water as soft as silk.

Scented bath oils and soaps can dry up skin, too: "The moment you put scent in an oil or a soap, it makes it very drying," says Countess Csaky. "If you want to get out of a bath without having made your skin dry, forget about all those pricey oils. And if you want to give your skin a real treat at bath-time, take a small bowlful of rough kitchen salt, damp and rub it all over your body — arms, legs, stomach, back, shoulders, wherever you can reach. Then put a tablespoon of olive oil in the bath-water, step in and rinse off the salt. Scoop up the oil which will lie on the water and rub it all over yourself. The salt is a wonderful skin treatment — cleans it, makes it very smooth and preserves it — and the oil is marvellously softening."

If, however, a deliciously-scented bath is your idea of heaven, there's still no need to lash out fortunes on commercial goodies. Some old-fashioned chemists — Savory & Moore of New Bond Street, for one — will sell you minute quantities of essential flower oils like Gardenia, Jasmine and Carnation from about thirty pence. Add a coffee-spoonful to a small bottle of sweet-smelling almond oil — very cheap, from any chemist; throw in a half a teaspoon of the shook-up mixture to your bath and the whole bathroom will fill up with the lovely expensive smell.

Olive oil and home-made flower-oil alike have one drawback: they leave the bath fearfully tacky and slippery. But if the commercial preparations leave it scoured clean — you can just imagine what they're doing to your skin...

MAKING UP

Women waste more money on make-up than any other single item of personal expenditure. We waste it on eyeshadows that we learn to hate, and foundation creams that turn out to be the wrong colour; on lipsticks that go blue on us, and mascara that make our eyes run; on blushers we never get to grips with, and pretty little pencils we can never master the knack of using. If we could have a fiver for every bit of make-up rotting unused in the bathroom cabinet, in fact, we could probably afford a whole new Yves St Laurent outfit.

Why so much waste?

Because we're completely bewildered, most of the time, by the staggering number and variety of the products, colours, techniques and make-up looks on offer to us. So just one sortie into the cosmetics bit of a department store — with its rows of rival experts all eyeing us hungrily — and we lose our heads completely. And nine times out of ten we end up wasting good money on a product that's no good to us at all — instead of the super new make-up that could help us look prettier, younger and modern.

How do you avoid this kind of waste — without paying through the nose for expert advice?

"Easy," says Mary Davis Peters cheerfully. "Learn from the experts. Cultivate an eye for what's happening in current make-up ideas. Study all those faces photographed huge and full-colour for the beauty pages of glossy magazines. They've been made up by the cleverest people in the make-up game. You can learn all you need to know from them — then experiment yourself with the make-up you already have."

Study the techniques, not the products credited, and don't be bamboozled by all those brand-names. Colour-printing is so unpredictable that half the time the make-up isn't even credited to particular firms till the proofs come up. So close your mind to the worry of whether you can actually afford Max Factor Geminesse Rosebery Red Enriched Creme Lip Colour or Ultima II Silvery Heather Super Luscious Creme Eyeshadow, and concentrate, instead, on what's happening where, in what colour.

Look where the blusher is going — and how much of it there is. What's happening to the eyes to make them look so huge and glittery? Colour all round? — or only halfway along the lower lid — or just on top? Pearly gleam on the eyebrow bone or not? Lots of mascara — or just a touch? And why doesn't that hard red lipstick look hard?

Because it's been glossed, probably.

When you come to experiment yourself, try to shed the cast-iron convictions you'll discover you tend to have about what you can or can't do to your own face. They're usually based on nothing more than habit.

"I can usually tell a woman's age by her eye make-up if by nothing else," says Joan Price. "Over forty-five. No eyeshadow and lots of dark brown or black eyeliner, painted on nice and hard along the top. Or maybe just a little eyeshadow — in a nice powder blue. But definitely nothing under the eyes. 'It makes me look tired,' they tell you. How do they know? They've never tried."

If you look carefully at the basic make-up in those beauty pictures, incidentally, you'll notice it's very cool looking and golden — the way most women's skins are naturally — and never one of those warm peachy orangey hues to which English women are so addicted — "that terrible brightness that stops at the chin," as Joan puts it.

An incidental bonus of these pale foundations is that it's almost impossible to go wrong when picking the shade — whereas even half a tone out in one of those bright pink or peachy shades means a totally wrong colour for you, and another pound or so down the spout. Pink and peach always change colour and go orange on the skin. Choose a putty tone instead.

By the same token, bright orange and peach-pink face-powders are also out of favour:

most professional make-up artists prefer a light dusting of a neutral or translucent powder.

All the colour on the face is added afterwards, in the shape of what our mothers used to call plain rouge — but which today are shapers, shaders, blushes, blushers, Cheek Glow or whatever. You can use a cream or liquid form, and put it straight onto your base: or you can powder first, so that your face has an even, interesting pallor all over, and then start adding colour in powder form, with a great big brush. This kind of colour is used fairly boldly today — no longer just a discreet natural-looking blush; which is all the more reason why it needs to be applied carefully, and softly blended in. Make-up artists — a whole new profession today, they call themselves *visagistes* — often use two or three different colours: a slightly browny one in the hollow of the cheek to give a little shape to the face — though not the gaunt hungry look of a few years back; and then a brighter pink or coral colour further up and ivory highlighter near the eyes.

Any woman can pick a lipstick for herself with a fair degree of confidence — it's eye make-up that's so dreadfully confusing. Pencils and brushes and crayons, liners and shadows and gleamers and shiners and glossers and highlighters — it's all mind-boggling stuff. Here are the facts to guide you through the maze. There are basically four different kind of eye-colour you can apply to the area around your eyes. There's CREAM shadow which you smear on with your fingertip or apply with tiny little sponges. The newest are water-based and oil-free, so that they won't melt or collect in little lines in the creases of the eye. *Visagistes* often use a gleamy white, beige or even pink cream over the whole eyelid area as base before they get going on the colour. There's POWDER shadow, put on with a brush, a finger or a little sponge again. There's LINER that you paint on with a small brush: but you can forget this one for the time being, since nobody bothers with it much at the moment. And finally there are PENCILS, often called CRAYONS, which you use for an accurate application of colour.

The great pencil-mania of a couple of years back — when absolutely all the colour on your face was pencilled on to it — is subsiding now, but pencils are still a good way to get the colour exactly where you want it: in the crease of your lid or run in a soft blur round the lashline instead of a hard painted-on line. Don't buy a pencil without trying it: Some pencils are so hard that you can wreak horrible damage on the delicate skin around your eyes by dragging them across it: if so, throw them away. And most model girls, we notice, soften pencils before use by scribbling in the hollow of their warm hand with them first.

Much the best of the medium-priced bases, we've thought for years, is that runny stuff in the pale blue tubes made by Woltz. It's liquid, it's thin, it comes in lots of good colours including very pale neutral ones, it's feather-light, it gives you a lovely glow — and it still manages to do an efficient cover-up job on minor blemishes. (Shirley Conran remembers going to a press reception and being much struck by how wonderfully good and glowy all the fashion ladies looked. It turned out that they'd all been to a Woltz party that morning and were trying out the make-up. Honestly!)

Particularly good value are the Miss Selfridge range — beautifully packaged and always bang up to date with colours and technical detail. For under two pounds they sell a Brush-Tidy with a full range of different-sized brushes and little sponge-tipped sticks; they sell all the brushes on their own, too, including the big soft ones for blushers for about thirty-five pence. They do a marvellous kajal pencil for black lining inside the lashes; they do big two-tone pencils — a different colour each end — in all the up-to-the-minute colours for about fifty pence; and to keep your face-pencils sharpened, they do big bright-coloured pencil-sharpeners that take small or large pencils for about twenty-one pence.

Otherwise, head for your friendly local Woolworths or Boots. Rimmel and Evette, Outdoor Girl and Miners between them will have most of what you're looking for — everything except the very latest fashion-fad in colour. Bright young *visagiste* Sara gave us a rundown on some of the bargains she rates.

"Absolutely no need to waste money on things like eyebrow pencils or blushers," she said briskly. "There are plenty of great colours in the cheaper ranges. Rimmel, for instance, have splendid colour blushers — quite as good as products at three times the price; and Miners have more good colours — they're very quick off the mark, too, with exciting new colours. Evette have some very good cosmetic brushes — a quite big very cheap one for a blusher, very important to good make-up. I'm never without one."

"And my own favourite economy tip? Why spend good money on expensive powder? I find that Johnsons's Baby Powder, lightfly dusted over your foundation, works quite as well."

All you need is a Good Cut

All you need is a GOOD CUT

"Take Madam away and get that common colour out of her hair," said the hairdresser, disdainfully flicking the new client's hair with his finger tips.

And did Madam fling off the unbecoming pink nylon robe and walk out, declaring she hadn't come here to be insulted? Of course she didn't. Demoralised, she cringed off to the backwash, murmuring apologetically about how the sun always turned her hair that awful colour and, no doubt, she tipped everyone lavishly: "Oh thank you...thank you so much...it's lovely...thank you..." and then bankrupted herself for a month over the bill.

Why do we do it? Sit marooned with magazines and a damp neck while the hairdresser lies: "Just another two minutes..." as he moves, scissors poised, towards a lady with shoulder-length hair? Pay a fortune for a finger-full of conditioner? Go through the dreadful embarrassment of tipping ten pence here and thirty pence there and· "Will you give this to Christine for me?" and the worry of whether to give Paul one pound or fifty pence and finally wedging the compromise seventy-five pence into his tight jeans' pants' pocket, knowing that he'll be driving home in his Lotus while we're still queueing for the Number 9?

We do it because shiny, well-groomed hair is the most valuable fashion asset a girl can have. She can get away with old boots and a too-short skirt if her hair is stunning, but she might as well wear a housefrock from the Bargain Basement as her new Ossie if her hair is a lacklustre mess or set into a stiff, out-dated bouffant.

Hair is the instant give-away; of taste, money and age. A cheap hair-do almost always looks it and nothing widens the generation gap more for the forty-year-old than an insistance on those dear little girlish flick-ups her husbands and friends found so enchanting fifteen years ago.

DO WE REALLY HAVE TO SPEND A BOMB ON IT?

Providing you actually do go to the hairdresser for your hair and not for a lovely, gossipy chat or because you need a professionally sympathetic ear for your troubles — in which case a psychiatrist at ten pounds an hour works out cheaper as he doesn't have to keep dashing off to massage somebody else's ego when he's in the middle of doing yours — you can achieve the same look for the price of a good cut.

First you've got to find a hairdresser who will give you manageable, trouble-free, drip-dry hair. Preferably the sort that never ever needs setting.

HOW TO LOCATE HIM?

Study the heads and faces around you, bearing in mind it's no good coveting a shiny, short style on a jolly looking round-faced girl if you've got naturally curly hair, a flat crown and a long jawline. Even strangers are usually flattered to be asked who does their hair and be sure to get the name of the stylist, too, since tastes and talents differ in every salon.

Hang around outside likely looking hairdressers and decide which salon turns out the nicest hair, then go in and book an appointment. The man — or woman — you want is probably the one who can't take you until next Thursday at three forty-five and not the one who can fit you in now. The trick is to sneakily read the appointment book upside down and go for the stylist with the most solid black under his name.

Talk to him before you go to the backwash, when your hair looks its scruffiest and tell him what you're after. Ask advice but don't be browbeaten into the newest, obligatory shape which could need professionally trimming every few weeks. It's noticeable that those heroic ladies who come back from six months up the Amazon looking as though they have just stepped out of Leonard's usually have essentially simple hairstyles.

Journalist Penny Vincenzi, who was recently the beauty editor of *Honey,* has super straight curtains of dark hair and a long fringe. "Any fool can manage this style," she says. "I go to the hairdresser once a year and have six inches cut off it and that's it. Perhaps you'd better say twice a year because it's meant to be terribly bad for the split ends but I can't say I've noticed them myself. I cut the fringe and henna my hair about twice a year, which tones in the odd grey bits and gives red highlights, rather than the chic, plummy hairdresser look. Shampooing? Oh, I just wash it in the bath once a week with whatever the children have left over and let it dry itself."

LEARN TO LOVE WHAT YOU'VE GOT

It's a fact of life that all curly heads yearn for a straight, Mata Hari bob and girls with straight hair invest heavily in heated rollers and perms. Anything involving straightening or curling is going to cost in cash and upkeep, so get a cut that realistically takes account of your hair type and texture. If your hair is naturally thin you can treat it with Thicken Hair, have it cleverly layer cut for underneath body and it still won't hold a bouncy style for long.

Same thing applies if you demand a carbon copy of a model girl's hairstyle in one of the glossies. Maybe it won't suit your type of hair and anyway, those definitely *Now* cuts in magazines are designed to look great until the camera clicks and not to last for months.

Keep a keen eye on what's happening. Which way does the hairdresser lift the hair as he blow-dries it? Where are the rollers going and what size are they? Armed with a few tricks of the trade you'll only need to have a dry trim at future appointments.

Don't accept rinses or any other little extra unless you actually need it; you've been living with your hair for years and should know if it needs a colour lift. And beware of any salon that automatically directs jets of sticky lacquer at every head. Lacquer is not only hell to get out, it's also the classic way of disguising a lousy cut.

If, at the end of it all, you aren't absolutely delighted with John's work and notice that Christopher is giving another lady the exact cut you fancied for yourself, don't hesitate to change around next time. After all, you're the client.

DON'T OVERLOOK AFTER-HOURS HAIRDRESSING

All salons have teaching sessions for their juniors one or two evenings a week and they've got to have somebody to practise on. Not as drastic as it sounds at a good salon since a senior stylist is always on hand with advice and the juniors are, at the very least, anxious to please and succeed. Hairdressing schools are another good source for free or nearly-free hair-do's but we'd be inclined to go for the very best salons. After all, their juniors have been watching experts at work. A friend of ours was so pleased with her after-hours hairdressing that she stuck with the junior through her training and now pays for the same service that she used to get free.

YOU'VE GOT THE CUT SO WHAT DO YOU DO NOW?

As little as possible. The less you muck about with your hair, the better the condition. Straightening with chemical straighteners and bleaching are a great way of damaging the shafts of the hair and splitting ends but, no matter what your mother may have told you, they don't cause lasting damage. New hair keeps on growing. Any kind of traction is much more serious as you can damage the roots, so don't yank away with a stiff brush to straighten out waves and kinks and don't sleep in tight rollers. As if you would.

Healthy hair could be as much a result of what you eat as what you put on it, so have lots of fruit, salads, protein and drink plenty of water which will be nice for your figure, too. Highly spiced foods and fats don't do much for hair or complexion and insisting on a regime of one hundred strokes a day may be character forming for you but it's positively harmful for your hair.

Use the softest possible bristle brush to just smooth down the hair, and a saw-cut comb with extra wide teeth, rather than one of those moulded plastic combs which have sharp bits on the side

to jag the hair. Those slim, little brushes with a one-inch circle of bristle at one end are super for curling back short ends (Kent do a good one) and you'll need a light, easy-to-hold hair dryer to blow wet hair into a swinging shape or do a quick revival job in the mornings. Most of the new hair dryers have a switch for alternative voltages so you won't need to fiddle about with adaptors and risk fusing the whole hotel when you're abroad. The skill in blow-drying lies in rolling hair firmly around the brush from the roots, up and away from the scalp. Regular jets of very hot air or continuous use of heated rollers are a rotten idea unless you like your hair looking hay dry.

ARE YOU WASTING MONEY ON SHAMPOOS?

No matter what miracles the label on the bottles proclaim, shampoos do not differ all that much. Either they are detergent based and strong, or soap based and mild and harder to wash out.

Boots Family Shampoo works out nine times cheaper than some of the luxury ones containing Alpine herbs or whatever the currently fashionable additive may be, and it's just as effective.

Some detergent shampoos are stronger than others, and most of the ones labelled "For Greasy Hair" are very strong indeed and would be excellent for washing up. If you've got greasy hair you would probably do better to use a milder, "Dry Hair" shampoo, wash your hair every few days and even use a little conditioner. Gloss is not, after all, the same thing as grease.

There's no real cure for dandruff but you can keep it under control by regular washing or by using a shampoo containing Selenium Sulphide or Zinc Pyrithione, like Head and Shoulders Lotion, Revlon ZP11 and Selsun.

Dandruff is often an excessive shedding of old skin, due to various metabolic changes in the body generally. Philip Kingsley, a registered trichologist, says that stress particularly causes changes in skin secretions and makes dandruff a lot worse. He cites the story of a famous actor whose dandruff disappears completely when he's relaxing on holiday but reappears disastrously when he's before the cameras or starting a new play. Mr. Kingsley has some delightfully economic ideas about hair care: "The more expensive shampoo isn't necessarily the best," he says. "Really, the ideal shampoo is one you can make yourself. Get half a kilo of green soft soap, dissolve it in about one litre of distilled water and heat it until it dissolves. Let it stand for a couple of days, until the sediment has gone to the bottom, pour off the clear stuff and use that. Like all soap based shampoos it does tend to stick a bit in very dry or bleached hair, but in that case you should finish off with a vinegar or lemon rinse. This type of shampoo makes the hair much easier to manage than a detergent based one."

WHICH CONDITIONERS?

The two commonest kinds are the rich, wax based or oily treatments for dry and damaged hair, and those useful "cationic" conditioners which control the static electricity in fly-away hair which may be caused by central heating, nylon brushes and combs or even the kind of shampoo you use. You can often get wholesale sized and priced pots of Estolan for the dry hair treatment, and this is good stuff if your hair is going to take a bashing from the elements. We find Toni's Tame does tame a treat, but everyone has their own favourites amongst the "smoothers". Study the small print on the bottle and experiment to find which conditioner is best for you.

Mr Kingsley says he's rather anti conditioners, feeling that healthy hair shouldn't need them and doesn't reckon on the traditional olive oil, hot towel routine because you have to use so much shampoo getting out the sticky oil that you undo all the good you might have done: "It's a better idea to drop an egg on your hair, massage it in and wash it off and, if you're going out in the hot sun you could massage in a little almond oil. It's more expensive than olive oil but doesn't go rancid and smell nasty."

DO YOU NEED TO SPEND EIGHT POUNDS OR SO EVERY FEW WEEKS ON COLOUR?

Somebody came up to Molly Parkin the other day outside a Tesco in Cornwall and said, "God! Your hair looks good!" and Molly smirked proudly, reflecting that it had cost her around ninety pence instead of the eleven pounds she previously paid to get her roots redone.

When Molly lived in London she had her hair dyed a bright, startling green by Regis, the visagiste at the sadly defunct Biba Beauty Salon. Small boys used to follow her in the streets calling out, "What's happened to your hair, then?" and at parties her emerald hair was an instant conversation stopper and starter. When she moved to Cornwall, Molly rightly presumed that she would be unlikely to find such an adventurous hairdresser in her village, so she went along to the local chemist and chose herself a glorious, glossy, black shampoo-it-in permanent tint. "Oh, I wouldn't have *that* colour, it doesn't look very natural," said the assistant who didn't know Molly. In fact, Molly did not actually do her own hair colour. The last time we saw artist Patrick Hughes, Molly's husband, he had raven black finger nails. He had forgotten to put on the plastic gloves that are supplied with the hair colour.

In the old days even quite nice ladies, who happened to be moving to another town or salon could be seen bribing juniors for the magic "$\frac{1}{4}307/0 + 308/0 + 30$ vol. drop of 40" formula which was the secret of their "natural" blonde hair. Actress Georgina Hale once paid her own fare back from the States to get her roots redone at the Ginger Group. Colourists were *that* important.

Not any more. Now we don't care if hairdressers guard their little colour cards as though they were the gold in Fort Knox because we can do without them and do it ourselves. And it only takes us half an hour.

The secret of successfully colouring your own hair is to imagine you're dying a shirt. You can't dye a black shirt yellow unless you bleach out the black first. You can turn beige into a nice chestnut, but haven't a hope of instantly dyeing a chestnut skirt beige. Same with hair. It may be tempting to suddenly, startlingly change into a scarlet woman or a platinum blonde bombshell but anything involving bleaching is better left to the professionals, and dramatic changes of hair colour do have a way of showing you up at the roots.

Basically there are five ways to add colour to your hair (or, indeed, remove it) and, no matter which you choose, be sure to try a strand test first and follow the instructions on the bottle to the letter.

Temporary Rinses won't change your hair colour. They are the ones that give dull hair a sparky lift or tone down the brassiness in bleached hair. Hairdressers invariably use them when they haven't got your colour quite right. "We'll just put on a little ash after the final wash and it will be perfect!" Most temporary rinses contain a setting agent as well and we've tried, and particularly approve, Twice as Lasting and Wella Colour Set.

Semi Permanent Rinses are usually only mild colourants although some of them do include a bleaching solution which makes them, correctly, neither *semi* permanent nor a rinse. If you ever have to mix two things together then be sure there's peroxide or a similar, penetrating bleacher in there somewhere. Don't expect too much of the semi permanents. They don't cover up grey and the colour does tend to disappear in the wash. They could be a good beginning if you're only after the slightest variation on your own colour or are chicken about anything absolutely permanent. Good ones are L'Oreal's Colour Glo, Polycolor and Polyglow and Elida's Sea Witch.

Permanent Tints: These are magic. Shampoo in the tint, leave it for twenty minutes and that's it. They are often called rinses which, of course, they are not or they wouldn't be permanent. It's probably a hangover from the days when it wasn't done to change your hair colour. "Oh it's just a rinse," you said as you miraculously changed from mouse to glowing chestnut. They do alter the pigment of the hair and cover up grey marvellously. Again, you can't turn yourself dazzling blonde if you are a beautiful brunette (who wants to, anyway?) unless you go through the bleaching routine first, but

boring browns can lighten and brighten themselves up and there is the most marvellous choice of subtle shades. We've only got two carps but both of them, we've found, apply to professionally coloured hair, too. Blondes and beiges may go a bit brassy after the second or third wash and will need toning down with a silver or ash rinse. And you *do* need to use a conditioner after colouring even though some of the products make a big thing about their built-in conditioners. We've tried nearly all the permanents and reckon Toni's Casual and Revlon's Colorsilk have the best range of colours.

Bleaches frighten us. They vary from the fierce ones that can change you from black to blonde to the milder kind that simply lift the hair colour a shade or two. Either way, there's a possibility of overdoing the bleaching process and coming out like yellow wire wool. Belle Blonde is a mild lightener with a 'booster' sachet enclosed for the daring. Clairol's Born Blonde can be used in conjunction with their Born Blonde Colourant to give you the exact shade of blonde you fancy, and Inecto's Hi-Lite is an extra strong one.

Highlights: We think the nicest way to use bleach is for highlights. This used to involve covering up your hair with a plastic bath hat, pricking pins into it, pulling out bits of hair with a hairpin or crochet hook and bleaching them. A bit of a fuss and that's why we're sold on Clairol's hair-painting kit, Quiet Touch. With this, you just mix up the formula and paint in the highlights. Get a natural effect by painting lots of mixture on to thin strands of *underneath* hair; that way, the unpainted hair will fall lightly over the highlights and you won't get a visible root problem. Pin-curl up the top hair while you're painting, so it's well out of the way. Quiet Touch is a mild bleach so it only works on light brown to blonde-ish hair; well, nobody with dark hair should streak it, anyway, unless they like to look as though they have gone prematurely grey.

Henna is the stuff for brunettes. It's just natural henna leaves ground into a powder and, depending how long you leave it on, it turns your hair a rich, glossy, red-brown or merely adds rich, glossy reddish highlights. All that rich and glossy bit happens because henna is a super conditioner, too. Don't, repeat don't, use henna on bleached hair or on hair that could, by any stretch of the imagination, be described as "fair", or you will go a nasty, hard orange colour.

It does wash out a bit, in which case you can use a henna rinse (both basic henna and the rinse are now obtainable at most chemists and, if you can't get them locally, write to the Culpeper herbal people whose address is in the LOOK IT UP HERE chapter at the back of the book) and it does stain. Not just your hair but your face, your hands, your bathroom, your family, anything it touches. So, before you start, be sure to drape you and your home in old towels

and newspapers and wear rubber gloves.

How to do it? Long hair needs around four ounces, short hair about two and a half ounces. Put the henna powder in an old saucepan, add boiling water gradually, mixing to a smooth, slightly runny paste about double cream thick. Leave it to cool. Re-heat and add the juice of half a lemon and a teaspoon of vinegar.

Working on dry hair, start applying the henna near the scalp, making a parting and putting on the paste with a tinting brush or a flat, oilpainting brush. Go on making partings, a quarter of an inch higher or lower, again and again and again. It's messy and it drips but try and remember you're saving yourself at least ten pounds on the professional job.

It gets easier as the hair gets wetter and, when you're doing the back, make horizontal partings and brush the henna along, working from the top downwards. Nearly finished. Work the remaining henna on to the ends of your hair with gloved hands and plaster it close to your head. Now, put on a hair-net like Ena's, top it with a tightly fastened plastic bag and cover the lot with an old towel. The idea is not to frighten your children and alienate your husband, but to generate and retain heat, which is what makes the colour take. The darker the hair, the longer you should leave it on. Could you stand six hours?

Shampoo out the henna and rinse and rinse — for at least ten minutes. At the end of all that you deserve the gloriously coloured and conditioned hair you will certainly have.

STRAIGHTENING AND PERMING

Must you? Really? Oh well then, if you can't stand those wirey curls another minute it's a cunning idea to give yourself a home perm. This sounds crazy but the idea is to smooth the hair rather than curl or straighten it. Chemical straighteners are stronger than a perm solution and, therefore , potentially more damaging to the hair; they are also extremely difficult to use and, unless you're an expert you'll probably give youself nice straight ends and kinky bits next to the scalp. Just apply the perm solution and then roll your hair around giant, at least three-inch-wide, rollers. You can't buy these in England yet, so either use two jumbo-sized ones together or, better still, punch holes in a plastic bottle and cut it into roller-size chunks. Leave the underneath curly so it provides body for the smooth top hair and you've got a good, basic shape.

Home perms are gentler than they used to be but just as tricky to set unless you are very clever at managing rollers and a bit of a contortionist, too. Enlist the help of a nimble-fingered friend.

The less perming you do the better and, if you've got the sort of straight hair that spikes out in all directions, we're in favour of end-curl-only perms rather than the whole head job. Toni and Elida both do them. If you've given yourself a whole head perm it can look even lovelier when it

has half grown out.

Sandra Leamon, who is a Creative Director of a big advertising agency and pretty creative with her own looks, too — her specs make Elton John's look prosaic — has her hair permed all over into a lovely, wild freak-out. Then, as the perm grows out she just parts her hair in the middle, sticks a couple of slides in each side and lets the remaining permed bits hang down in ringlets, giving her the look of a lovable and appealing spaniel. This way she only needs to pay for a perm twice a year and her hair is always in good condition.

HOLIDAY HAIR needs even more loving care than you give your body. It's amazing the amount of people who lavish sun oil on their skin and just leave their hair to got ruined. Hot sun, strong winds and salt water dry out the hair and accentuate split ends. So, get your hair well cut before you go away. Condition it regularly, whether it's dry or greasy. Always rinse it after you've been in pool or sea and, if it is at all bleached, try and keep it covered up to avoid the inevitable brassiness that comes out with the sun. Prudent false blondes always travel with a beauty case full of ash or silver rinses.

COVER IT UP

If you still can't do a thing with your hair after all this good advice, then do what the model girls do and cover it up. Not with a wig; wigs were okay in the days of the "bounced-up bouffant" when they didn't really show and hair-pieces used to be great for thickening up that 'sixties style deliberately dishevelled mop, but today any false hair tends to look as though you are concealing a clinical case of alopecia.

Get clever with scarves. For instance, use a great big cotton one (silk slips), tie it at the back, tuck the triangle point under like a snood, twist the remaining long ends round and round into a rouleau and wind them around your head. Very chic.

Or you could just invest in a Gucci, tie it under your chin in the tradional British way, and look as County as the Queen at a point-to-point.

Mini-Marketing

MINI-MARKETING

(Or never Buy The Giant Economy Size If They Sell It In 4oz Packets)

How many times recently have you gazed pensively into your purse or surreptitiously sifted through your pockets, looking for the pound note you knew you had somewhere?

"Where does it go?" we keep sobbing and the answer could be on a tube of toothpaste, a packet of cigarettes and three stamps which don't seem like *shopping* but, nevertheless, add up to one pound plus. We've turned into a nation of Remember When bores, remembering when butter was ten pence a half pound, the weekend joint cost less than a pound and ten pounds was a reasonable sum to budget for the weekly housekeeping expenses.

With food bills rising some thirty per cent annually and hidden expenditures like shoe-mending and dry-cleaning now costing much the same as a new pair of shoes or a new dress did a few years ago, there's got to be some way of staying solvent without lowering standards to the baked-bean level.

MAKE LISTS

An intensely boring occupation but the only sure way to control spending. Every time you go out shopping, make a list of *exactly* what you need and don't allow yourself to be side-tracked by a Special Offer Giant Economy Pack of something you don't need this very minute, or seduced by a sudden sighting of out-of-season cherries.

This sort of mini-marketing takes time but it isn't as tough on the arm muscles as a weekly shop and, because you're always in and out of the shops, you know exactly what is currently cheap and in season and thus, you eat better for less money.

To the supermarket-trolley shopper, fresh pineapples and peaches, for instance, are a luxury so they pay the high prices, buy tinned or do without. Regular market-browsers know that there are times when giant pineapples are as little as twenty-five pence each (lovely, dotted with sugar and Kirsch) and peaches sell for as little as six for ten pence (delicious skinned, sliced, covered with thick cream and demerara and quickly caramelised under the grill).

If you still seem to be overspending at an alarming rate, try writing down every single purchase for a month and see where you can make savings. Did you really need that branded soap when Boots and Woolworth sell packets of four at almost the same price as the one? Are the pets over-eating? Or, putting it more kindly, wouldn't it be wiser to feed them butcher's scraps mixed with dried-in-the-oven wholemeal bread leftovers, rather than the expensive tinned doggy foods?

NEVER GO SHOPPING WITH MORE MONEY THAN YOU NEED

Sure as anything, if you've got an extra fiver floating about in the back of a wallet, or a fat new cheque book, you'll be tempted by a pot of luxury cream you fleetingly believe is going to erase every line from your face, or a curious novelty like Garlic Flavoured Croutons which you could easily make yourself in about five minutes. With a limited supply of cash in hand you've just got to shop economically.

Every now and again check those long supermarket bills

against the goods. The cashiers aren't out to cheat you but they are only human with brains that once in a while will fail to pass on the right messages to the fingers; we've spotted four mistakes in the last couple of months, adding up to some three pounds. And try not go food shopping when you're hungry. Harold Wilson says his holiday home in the Scilly Isles is stockpiled with tinned goods he bought when he was ready for lunch. The best possible time to shop for the evening meal is when you have just eaten a substantial meal and won't fall on everything with drooling taste buds.

There's a feeling around that if you buy lots of something at a time you automatically get it cheaper. Not true, unless you happen to be a wholesaler or a retailer.

BULK BUYING SAVES TIME BUT NOT NECESSARILY MONEY

The Cash and Carries who admit the general public are usually situated out of towns and, quite rightly, reckon they are providing a service for people who don't live near a shopping centre and who might otherwise have to drive miles every time they run out of sugar. They offer bulk-buy convenience rather than cheap goods and although their prices will probably be more competitive than the village shop, they won't differ greatly from a High Street supermarket.

If you find household shopping

a bore and a chore you can get everything, bar the perishables, from a bulk-buy mail order firm. They make shopping as easy as doing the laundry list but be prepared to empty the spare room or move the car out of the garage to store the obligatory case-loads of stuff. And the idea of eating your way through a seven-pound pack of raspberry blackmange powder may make you heave a bit.

They don't claim to cut prices, either. How can they when they have to cover the costs of handling, packaging and delivery? But they do go on a lot about saving time and nervous energy and the advantages of stockpiling goods as a hedge against inflation.

The idea is to buy 144 rolls of loo paper and then sit back, smiling complacently, watching shop prices rise monthly. It's a good idea, though to check local prices before writing your cheque. If the same thing is cheaper down the road it's not much point quaintly storing twelve dozen Andrex under the bed. Really compulsive bulk buyers might get a better financial deal filling up the car boot from a street market, cut price shop or supermarket.

CAN ANYONE GET INTO THE WHOLESALE CASH AND CARRIES?

These are the real money-savers and although it's sometimes possible to pass yourself off as a bona-fide trader, most wholesale warehouses have become very fierce about credentials. Not surprisingly, small traders kicked up a fuss; they were finding competition from the multiples and supermarkets tough enough without their customers getting in on the act, too.

A couple of years ago, the wife of an eminent lawyer went to the trouble of having cards specially printed "The Johnston-Smythe Catering Company" — which was sufficient, then, to get her an official, numbered retailer's card at her local wholesaler. She says she found the biggest savings were on things like J-Cloths, jams and saucepans. "I shared out some of the shopping with friends because twenty-four boxes of corn flakes are too many corn flakes even for a large family and a dozen pots of Marmite do go on a bit."

Recently, she had to renew her card and was asked to flourish a VAT number, receipts and other evidence of her authenticity as a trader, so she retired graciously, much to the relief of her husband who had lived in fear of meeting his wife across a crowded courtroom when she was brought up for false pretences. She was, she says, sad rather than resentful when the bonanza ended. "It's not the fantastic savings I miss because, somehow, it didn't work out all that much cheaper, but the bliss of doing three months' shopping in an hour."

DO YOU KNOW HOW LITTLE FAIRY LIQUID WILL DO THE WASHING UP IN YOUR SINK?

You're unlikely to find out if you've got a dozen or more bottles of the stuff in a cupboard.

The reason most of us don't save on bulk buying, even at wholesale prices, is simply psychological. The disadvantage of laying in vast quantities of cheap plonk is that you *drink* vast quantities of cheap plonk which may be very jolly but doesn't cut back on the bills.

The mother who lets her children crunch through half a dozen bags of crisps and a pack of biscuits at a single sitting of Dr Who is *not* the lady who has to dip into her purse for the ready cash, but the one with the comforting fantasy that all those cases of crisps and biscuits in the garage are free.

WHO SELLS WHAT CHEAPEST AND NICEST?

Even those of us who enjoy shopping don't usually have the time — or the inclination — to go ferreting from shop to shop finding out whose sugar is two pence a pound cheaper today and which store is beguiling us with a loss leader (a cut-price come-on).

A store's own brand usually works out anything from two to six pence cheaper than the well-known branded equivalent and, as *Which*, the Consumer Guide, pointed out when they covered grocery prices, the quality is much the same.

They reckoned that ASDA (a Midlands and Northern group of mostly superstores) have the cheapest own-brands or cut-price alternatives to the branded goods and that Safeway, Allied Suppliers and Tesco are the cheapest of the chains with branches in most areas.

If you're after brands, then ASDA and William Jackson (another mainly Northern group) are the cheapest with some of their brands actually costing less than other chains' own brands. Of the chains to be found almost anywhere, Safeway, Allied Suppliers and Tesco are again the cheapest, along with Woolworth.

Waitrose have the widest choice of brands *and* own brands, Sainsbury offer a particularly large range of own brands and Mac Markets, Safeway and Tesco have the widest choice of brands.

Which did this investigation a few years ago but their findings still seem to us to apply, and shopping around the chains and multiples we've discovered still other advantages of spreading your custom about a bit, rather than buying everything from one place.

British Home Stores are renowned for superb British cheeses and some of the larger Woolworth branches have a wider and more esoteric selection of foreign cheeses than a top-class delicatessen.

Dewhurst, a butcher with branches all over the country, always seem to stock the cheapest frozen chickens around. Simmer a chicken with lots of vegetables and herbs and you'll easily get two meals out of a three to four pound bird for a family of four, plus a lovely soup.

Safeway, Waitrose and Sainsbury are good value for New Zealand lamb, and, if you marinade chops in lemon juice and herbs or spike a roast with bits of garlic and rosemary, it's hard to tell the cheap foreign animal from the expensive English one.

Safeway appear to be the only chain where you can regularly buy loose beansprouts. Saute them gently in a little oil with some sliced celery, cabbage, mushrooms and cooked pork, dot the lot with soya sauce and children will fall on them with the enthusiasm they usually reserve for Chinese take away.

Waitrose are the place for an interesting variety of meat and fish and their herrings, already dipped in oatmeal, are especially nice and cheap.

Sainsbury and Waitrose both do excellent frozen kipper fillets. For a super first course, just skin the fillets, cut them into bite-sized pieces, marinade them in lemon juice, black peppercorns and a few crumbled bay leaves, and add a little olive oil at the last minute.

Sainsbury do have an irritating way of presuming you *know* that chicken livers or whatever it is you happen to want that day, only come in on Thursdays. And Marks & Spencer have an even more vexing habit of quite often having nothing on their food shelves at all. Presumably their policy of selling only the freshest food makes them over-anxious about over-stocking. But both these stores sell their own-brand frozen orange juice cheaper than most, and, although Marks & Spencer's fresh food is usually very expensive, their American-style hamburgers, made with minced best steak, are as succulent as rare fillet at half the price. As for their steak and kidney puddings, there's so much meat in them they have to be the best and cheapest convenience food there is.

Boots, incidentally, often have packets of herbs and spices at a fraction of the cost of those dear little jars which sit on a special rack. Save money and space by nailing screw-top jars to the underside of a kitchen shelf for your herb and spice collection.

DON'T PAY FOR PACKAGING

Everything is cheaper bought loose by the ounce or the pound and, if you live in London, you'll find that shops like Camisa in Old Compton Street not only sell herbs and spices loose with *whole* nutmegs and such but also have rough sea salt for a few pence and freshly grated Parmesan cheese. Their very reasonable home-made pasta puts spaghetti, lasagne and ravioli up into the dinner party class.

Some British Home Stores branches sell a wide variety of frozen food loose and, when fresh vegetables are scarce and expensive, frozen broad beans, cooked for a few minutes in a tablespoon of water, with an ounce of butter, a sliced onion and a spot of salt and black pepper, make a delicious alternative.

WHY DO LEMONS COST SIX PENCE EACH IN THE HIGH STREET AND ONLY TEN PENCE FOR FIVE IN THE MARKET?

Rates and rents can't make all that much difference. It's always a saving to buy fresh fruit and vegetables in a street market, and the choice and quality is usually better than in the average greengrocer's. The only stalls to avoid are the sneaky ones which dishonestly announce "Fresh Strawberries 200 Yards Ahead" all the year round. Well, they may *technically* be fresh — but just a little jaded, perhaps, after that long journey from Guernsey?

It is not, of course, thrifty to drive a couple of miles to drop two pence on two pounds of sprouts. We know of a rich lady who sent her chauffeur along to the market in the Rolls because the avocadoes were cheaper than at the grand store where she placed her food order. Even on a saving of twenty pence per avocado she was down on the deal.

Trading stamps? Take them as a bonus if you're shopping in that store anyway, but don't go out of your way or pay extra to get them. A lot of licking goes into getting one tea towel.

You can't haggle over the price of a cabbage, but when it comes to fridges, record players and the more expensive household purchases we seem to have entered a bargaining situation. The Arabs have done it for years and we recently heard one trying it unsuccessfully at Harrods, but most English people are diffident about leaning over a counter and asking for a discount. The surprising thing is that if you're offering cash, shops will sometimes drop their price. If any shop or store advertises that they accept American Express or a similar card, there's no harm in suggesting that if you pay with money rather than a card they pass on to you the percentage that they will be saving on the deal.

NOBODY SHOULD PAY THE MANUFACTURER'S RECOMMENDED SELLING PRICE WITHOUT SHOPPING AROUND

Since the end of resale price maintenance this usually means that the maker has suggested a price nobody is going to charge, anyway. Be very controlled about the astonishing reductions you're offered all round. Exciting red tickets stuck all over a window may indicate nothing more than that the shop has invested in a lot of red tickets and, after you've paid ten pounds under the "list" price for an Amazing! CUT PRICE! Bargain! BANKRUPT STOCK! washing machine, you could see it lurking, quite quietly in somebody else's window at forty pounds under the "list" price.

If, say, you are looking for a new refrigerator, go along to a store with a big selection, take a good look, read the catalogues, consult the salesman, decide what you want and then go home and shop around by telephone. Phone all the discount warehouses like Comet and Trident and the local discount shops in your area, compare prices, and be sure to find out if they have the exact model you require in stock. They often haven't and you can wait months for delivery. Lots of people don't realise that they have access to a Discount Club through their work, union, professional association or private club. Their saving of twenty per cent to thirty-five per cent sounds dramatic but could be less than you would get at a discount warehouse. The discount mail order firms are usually, but not always, marginally more expensive than discount warehouses and shops but are a good idea if you live miles away from anywhere and it's easier to shop by post.

DON'T OVERLOOK THE LOCAL SHOPS

These are sometimes cheaper than discount buying on certain items. After shopping around the cut-price, discount specialists in the Tottenham Court Road area for a Music Centre, a friend of ours got it cheaper at a suburban branch of Green's. What's more, when the machine developed a fault, they stunned the complaining purchaser with the magic words: "Don't worry, sir, we'll have that put right for you by tomorrow. We sold it to you so it's our responsibility."

This is, of course, a legal fact (Sale of Goods Act 1893) and if you do find the machine of your dreams in a discount warehouse, make sure, first, that there aren't going to be heavy delivery charges to cancel out the bargain price, and that they don't pull the one about it being

the responsibility of the manufacturer or his service agent to deal with any faults. It's up to the retailer to repair or replace faulty goods or give you a refund.

All the various branches of John Lewis consistently give good value and service, and if you live anywhere near any of their branches check them out before buying, because their prices are often competitive with discount warehouses and shops.

Their "never knowingly undersold" policy means that if you've bought something from them and then see it for less around the corner they will refund you the difference. Sometimes, they even lower their prices when they happen to spot a nearby bargain themselves. This happened when Argos, who sell discount through their catalogue, opened near the Oxford Street branch of John Lewis. On another occasion a girl bought a ludicrously cheap duvet from John Lewis, pounds cheaper than inferior quality ones everywhere else, and says that the department-manager nearly broke down as he sold it. Evidently somebody, somewhere had bought a job lot of the identical duvets and was selling them off cheap. The unhappy manager swore he was losing several pounds on his wholesale price.

Another likely area for spotting bargains is in the pages of newspapers and magazines. Their special offers of coffee makers, linens, crockery and so on are often good value and Londoners can get a further seven and a half per cent reduction on any offers in IPC magazines and newspapers by using their Staff Shopping Service at 65 Long Acre, WC2. The sales-ladies here very nicely don't seem to mind whether you're a staff member or not.

HOW ABOUT CREDIT?

Better not if you want to get the best possible price but an overdraft at the bank is probably the soundest bet. Cards like Access are a reasonable way of tiding you over until the ship comes in but you do have to repay fifteen per cent of your outstanding balance or six pounds a month (whichever is the greater) and they only give you about two months' free credit before the high interest rates begin. H.P. works out at more than you think because even if a firm only charges a low ten per cent you go right on paying that to the end, even though you may have paid off nearly the whole price of the goods. This makes the interest on what you originally borrow-ed nearer eighteen to twenty per cent. Perhaps you've got an in-dulgent parent?

Whatever it is you're consider-ing buying, it is worthwhile send-ing for a relevant issue of *Which* to find out what they recom-mend. You may not agree with their conclusions but, at the least, they advise about what is safest and cheapest.

The only trouble with con-sumer associations and societies and ministries and all the other worthies who act like kindly, reproving, know-best Aunties is that they rather take the joy out of shopping, making you feel guilty if you paid two pence a pound too much for tomatoes last week or bought an iron with an unmarked neutral terminal. And we think shopping should be fun, whether it's finding the latest, lovely sweater shape in C & A for less than a fiver or sweet, juicy little oranges for only ten pence a dozen on our favourite Berwick Street stall.

The Great Freezer Myth

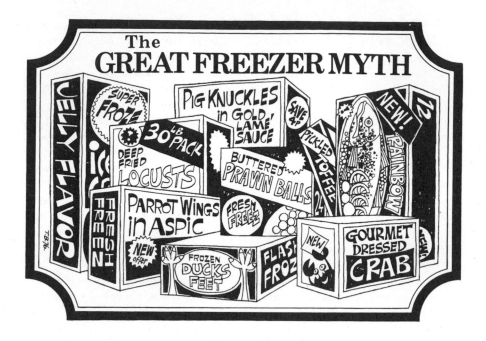

The GREAT FREEZER MYTH

If you happen to be a trained home economist with a hot line to Smithfield so you can check on fluctuating meat prices, have a husband who enjoys going out and shooting things and a garden just bursting with fruit and veg (*and* the time for all the necessary cleaning, parboiling and packaging of the home produced goods) then a freezer can help you eat better for less money.

For the rest of us, freezers are a waste of time and money and we can't understand why some four million people should want to eat frozen food all the year round, anyway. Presumably, all these canny freezer owners see themselves merrily dipping into their siege rations while the rest of us are petulantly paying two pounds fifty for a pound of stewing steak and queueing for fish fingers. At the very least they must believe they are saving money as they virtuously freeze

and stow.

BUT, THE NOTION THAT A FREEZER BRINGS THE HOUSEKEEPING BILLS TUMBLING DOWN IS ONE OF THE GREAT MARKETING MYTHS.

Take into account the depreciation of your capital outlay and the cost of the food and the machine, plus the price of electricity, insurance and maintenance and you've got to show a saving of around six pence per pound on everything in the freezer if you are to save money. And, unless you're very careful, a freezer can actually make you more extravagant.

There are all those new toys, for a start. A knife for slicing effortlessly through frozen meat, a thermometer to check you're not running the machine uneconomically cold, tinfoil containers, plastic bags and an electric machine to seal them tight shut, tie-tags if you haven't got a sealer, coloured labels, a special log book to note down dates so that no food is left in the freezer dangerously long and a pair of insulated gloves to save you freezing your fingers, too.

You don't really need a half of it. Just the plastic bags, the tie-tags (in different colours for quick identification), the knife and the thermometer. Instead of buying tinfoil containers, blasé freezer owners scrounge from friends who patronise the Chinese take away or buy big, square plastic bins of ice cream at Sainsbury. Not the round tubs, as they take up more room and space costs money. If you *must* seal up the plastic bags you can do it quite effectively with luke warm heated curling tongs.

Then, there's the lure of the Freezer Centres. These rows and rows of white chests seem to affect some women like being let loose in Harrods at sale-time with an account card. They go mad, lightheartedly chucking everything into their cleverly capacious trolleys, from Gourmet Dinners to Dressed Crab, because they imagine them to be bargains. In fact, even the special freezer packs of meat are not necessarily a saving. We've come across packs where, taking into account the cheaper cuts along with the lean and expensive bits, you're actually paying more per pound for a side of lamb than if you bought fresh meat from the butcher.

The error is to buy huge quantities of meat unless you are certain of your prices *and* your

butcher. After all, if one steak is tough the whole hindquarter of beef is going to be tough and you'd better like casseroles. Giant Economy Packs, produced by unknown manufacturers, are another snare. A mother, whose children are passionate about fish fingers, bought one of these anonymous packs which turned out so disgusting that even the fish finger addicts rejected them. She had to feed them to the cat.

And freezers hardly encourage thrifty meal planning.

If you haven't bothered to shop or don't feel like cooking a proper meal, there's no incentive to whip up a cheap omelette or do something creative with yesterday's left-overs. You dig a couple of steaks out of the freezer and, if you happen to have one of those giant packs of peas, you serve peas with the steak and finish the meal with ice cream. This diet is not particularly enticing or healthy and it costs more than fresh fruit and salads and greens.

HOW DO YOU MAKE A FREEZER PAY?

A girl we know is married to a keen allotment gardener which gives her a head-start and her freezer is always economically crammed to the lid: "In the summer it's usually three quarters filled with stuff from our allotment and in the winter this home grown food goes down to about one-third of the contents. That's our greatest saving."

She says the great freezer rule is to Eat One, Freeze One: "I've got into the habit of making two stews instead of one or slightly more pastry than I need, or whatever, and it works.

"You should always use the freezer for short term economies. If you're down in the country when there's a glut of something and they are practically giving it away, it doesn't take long to turn ten pounds of Bramleys into delicious apple purée. Brussels sprouts *always* go up just before Christmas, so last year I bought five pounds at ten pence a pound, washed and froze them (you don't need to blanch if they are to be eaten within a month) and then watched the price go up, up, up to twenty-two pence two days before Christmas.

"I use up all the oddments. If I have a pint of milk to spare I make, say, an onion sauce. And I always keep purée and sauces to turn into instant puddings and soups or to jolly up lamb chops for unexpected guests.

"I usually have a pastry binge when I make four pounds of pastry at a time and turn it into apple pies and quiches and raspberry flans. Then I buy a really good mince, one of the best buys at the freezer centres, and about once a month I give up a whole day to making shepherds pie, beef and carrot pie, stuffed cabbage leaves and stuffings, in different sized portions, for marrows and tomatoes."

Pamela Harlech says she used to be very snobby about freezers but now couldn't do without two in the country and one in London. "The thing is to use your freezer as an addition to fresh food rather than as an alternative," she says. "I buy up Welsh lamb at the end of June and July and put in salmon trout when they are cheap and, of course, game. August and September are my cooking months. I just cook and cook. Stews, soups, purées, Christmas puddings. Oh, I do all the cooking, though Nanny does sometimes help me shell peas. I always keep home-made spinach and artichoke soups, tomato and sorrel purées as a basis for soups and sauces — sorrel is delicious with salmon — and a bit of mousse. But, because I really prefer to cook things fresh, I generally do a fresh main course and take the soup and pudding from the freezer."

Lady Harlech says she finds frozen spareribs a splendid stand-by for unexpected guests. "If I hear that people are coming, I quickly stick the spare ribs on the boiler to defrost."

YOU HAVE TO BE VERY EFFICIENT, VERY ORGANISED TO RUN A FREEZER.

Some foods need part cooking, others have to be simmered or baked to the exactly right moment to keep the flavours intact.

Enzymes do go on working on frozen food so it's important to make sure nothing is left in long enough to deteriorate and give the family stomach ache. Ignore the imperious directive to LABEL CAREFULLY, imagining that it's a silly housewife who can't tell her chicken stock from her apple purée and you may find yourself having to dream up amusing puddings made from a basis of chicken bones. Once the freezer gets at it, all food

71

becomes an anonymous block.

When you've finished sucking the excess air out of your filled plastic bags with a straw ("No, darling, Mummy isn't playing, she's freezing a goulash...") are

you then prepared to put on an apron and play butcher's assistant to your husband as he tries to saw through the side of lamb you got cheap in the country last weekend?

FREEZERS ARE HARD WORK.

That Christmas advertisement showing a festive cracker showering out nasty skinless pork sausages and Cornish pasties with the command: *"Now's* the time to give your freezer a Christmas present..."* merely hints at the demanding character of a freezer. Okay if you're the calm sort who lifts the lid, notes there's nothing in the machine but the customary pig's head you've been going to turn into brawn "one day" for the past eighteen months and can just turn your back on it, but most freezer owners aren't like that. They have a compulsive obsession (as well as a purely practical reason) to keep the monster full.

Helen O'Leary, author of the useful *Career Girl Cookery,* has two children and a ten-year-old freezer. She says that after the Christmas holidays she phoned a friend to ask her to a peaceful, leisurely lunch. "I was amazed when she said she was far too busy cooking for the Easter holidays," says Helen. "Presumably so she could start her Christmas dinner in March. Freezer owners *always* seem to be working now to save time later. I can't understand why they can't save the time now and do the cooking later. Especially if they have got to be at home looking after the children, anyway. Incidentally, have you noticed how *bad* a freezer is for your figure? The foods that freeze really well are cakes and pastries and shepherds pie and steak and kidney puddings; all the weight-making bakes."

INSURE THE CONTENTS OF THE FREEZER

The Electricity Board cannot, alas, be relied upon to keep the supply of electricity going. Most people reckon they can just about withstand a twenty four-hour power cut but oh, the tension as they tear the duvets off the children's beds and tenderly wrap their machine to keep its temperature static; the agony of waiting the required time after the electricity has got going again before you can assess the damage. You can insure the food but the most depressing thing about finding that it has disintegrated into a soggy mess, is that you can't insure the woman-hours lost preparing it.

Dennis Norden has a lovely story about a man who came home from work and said to his wife, "What's for dinner, dear?" and she replied, "A boiling chicken, a duck, a couple of rabbits, some lamb chops, a side of beef, three steak and kidney pies, a little chicken paté, a few pizzas, a blackcurrant sorbet and half a dozen apple turnovers..." It could happen to you.

If freezers don't actually save time or money, then why are we buying them so avidly and patronising the one thousand or so freezer centres that have opened in the last few years? *Certainly not because frozen food is so delicious.*

In his book *Egon Ronay's Guide to the Best in Freezing,* Mr Ronay concluded that fresh food is nicer. He found that flavour and quality varied enormously amongst proprietory brands and starred Findus top for smoked haddock, Birds Eye for fish fingers and chips, Sainsbury for brussels sprouts and Kraft for beefburgers. The longer the storage, the greater the effect on flavour and texture, he warned, and pointed out that you never really know how long a frozen pizza has been sitting in the supermarket freezer when you buy it.

Caroline Conran, another stunning hostess and author of the inventive *Poor Cook,* says she thinks freezing ruins the taste of home-prepared food, too: "I must admit I don't like my freezer. I love the food when I'm cooking it, still love it when I put it in the freezer and then, somewhere between putting it in and taking it out I seem to lose contact with my cooking and I hate the food. It's not just that the flavour is impaired and the texture seems wrong; it's more that the whole joy of cooking is lost if you can't sit down and eat what you have made, there and then.

"I don't use my freezer intelligently and have absolutely never cooked anything specially for it. Somebody gave me a whole deer the other day and it would have been difficult managing that without a freezer, but when friends have given me pheasants and salmon trout, I've found that they taste really nasty after being in the freezer."

"I must say, I'm tired of going out to dinner with people who serve mushy soft fruits or strawberries with a chill inside that set the nerves jangling in your teeth and then say, 'Isn't it *marvellous* eating strawberries in December'," says Liza Kendall of *Vogue* magazine: "What's so marvellous about it if they taste absolutely filthy?"

Liza doesn't own a freezer, doesn't see the point as she lives right near Kensington High Street and uses the local shops and delicatessens as her freezer. "Though I can quite see that it would be useful if one lived miles away from anywhere in the middle of the country with a kitchen garden and lots of children."

WHAT IS THE RIGHT SIZE TO BUY?

If you've got the children and the kitchen garden, then most freezer owners swear that twelve cubic feet is the absolute minimum size to buy. A four cubic feet upright freezer is the smallest generally available and we think it's a pity you can't buy a tiny one point six cubic feet size to slot into a small corner of the kitchen, that will just take the necessities you can't buy fresh. As it is, you can only buy this small freezer as part of a refrigerator — sitting on top of the Indesit 225, for instance. Next time you buy a new fridge it's well worth considering one of these models that combines with the freezer.

Elizabeth David, that clever lady who taught a whole generation of Englishwomen to cook, uses her small freezer for storing stocks and broths, for her own bread, for herb butters, bunches of fresh tarragon for the winter and a supply of yeast. "Few people realise that fresh yeast can be frozen. It doesn't keep indefinitely, but it's useful to have a little to hand.

"If you're a good manager and a sensible shopper a deep freeze is of enormous value," she says. "Of course, if you stuff it full of expensive rubbish from a freezer centre you'll waste money and eat badly."

Cut-price Feasting

CUT-PRICE FEASTING

When you gather six jolly friends into your house for dinner they haven't, presumably, come to get drunk on your gin. Nor do they expect that you will have pawned the pearls in order to feed them on caviar and lobster. Nor will they rise and leave in a body if the wine served at dinner is Sainsbury's Second Best Plonk and your husband is unable to offer them brandy because it's now seven pounds a bottle.

In these lean times, guests are reasonable people: all we ask is that the company should be good, the drink just about drinkable, and the food perfectly delicious. One of the few nice things about the current crisis, indeed, is the way it's brought us all back to a realisation of what entertaining is basically about — seeing our friends and making them happy for as long as they're under our roof. Nobody's worried about impressing other people any more and the whole thing's much less of an effort. "Do you remember those dreadful little dinner-parties of the 'sixties?" said a friend with a shudder, "when we all used to make conversation instead of just simply chatting away and enjoying ourselves?"

Being more relaxed about it certainly doesn't mean not bothering. "Even when I was flat broke," says Avenger Girl Joanna Lumley," and all I could feed my friends on was heaps of rice and a few peanuts with a bit of onion, I've always had flowers on the table, even if it was only a newly opened buttercup. I buy glorious tall golden beige candles for about three pence each at a place I've discovered near Olympia (it's called the Lion's Den) and have masses of those. And my silver is always beautifully polished — no secret, just Silvo and hard work."

The other great hard-times

bonus is the way it has jacked up the general level of cooking. Now that we can't afford pricey convenience foods like smoked salmon and Parma ham, we're all turning ourselves, out of sheer necessity, into better and more imaginative cooks. "I've been saying so for ages," comments Robert Carrier. "It's the real silver lining to austerity." And we personally find cooking half the fun of entertaining.

THE SMALL DINNER PARTY

The great test of any cook's skill is, of course, the small dinner party where for much of the time everyone is actually sitting round the table concentrating on their plates. One hostess who is famous for the lovely lavish food at her dinner parties is Daria Schouvaloff, whose husband Alexander is director of the new National Theatre Museum. Eight people sit down to dinner, course after stunningly home-cooked course appears on the table, and Daria does all the food within a very strict budget of five pounds for eight people.

"To produce good food cheaply," she says, "you simply have to work at it. But I usually cook everything beforehand — I hate panics, and if you're badly held up in the kitchen, you can almost hear all your lovely kitchen economies draining away into glasses with another round of drinks."

"I begin by deciding what the main course is to be. Obviously it's got to be meat if it's at all a reasonable occasion, unless all your friends are vegetarian. Then it's very important to eat in sea-son all the way through — much nicer and much cheaper. Once I've calculated my central dish, I work out what I shall have left and plan accordingly. I almost always begin with soup. My father, who was French and very concerned about food, used to say that one should always start dinner with a soup — hors d'oeuvres are for lunch-time. Gentlemen always love soup, I notice, and they're impressed beyond measure by home-made soup. They love a pudding too — don't we all? — and most puddings work out fairly cheap. One of my most successful is Elizabeth David's Chocolate and Almond Cake, from her *French Provincial Cooking*.

"Typical menus? Well, one winter dinner started with a bland and creamy leek and potato soup, followed by a very peppery goulash with rice and a lettuce salad. Eggs were very cheap at the time, so I made a Creme Caramel as a pudding, then cheese. A summer menu began with a fresh light tomato soup — made when they were very cheap, or you can use tinned — then a rather extravagant veal stew made with mushrooms and served with rice, and for pudding an orange mousse — relatively cheap."

If even a fiver is more than you can run to, Chinese cooking is one answer. Nobody makes better and more economical use of their basic ingredients than the Chinese. Half a pound of meat stretches to feed six or eight people, with the vegetables lightly flash-fried in the same oil as the meat so that none of its goodness is wasted, and subtle spicy seasoning making the most of it all, with plenty of rice so that nobody's hungry. "When I was desperately poor, I was always giving Chinese dinners", says Shirley Conran. I made a whole thing about it, with proper rice bowls and chopsticks — they practically give them away in those Oriental shops and red paper-napkins. The food all came from the Chinese take-away if I was too tired to cook." You don't even have to offer wine with a Chinese dinner, moreover, lots of people actually prefer to drink the more appropriate China tea with it, just as you can legitimately offer lager instead of wine with an Indian dinner.

When people are really hungry, there's nothing they like better than simple, hearty food, ending up with a perfect pudding. Lord and Lady Tavistock love to get away from the formal splendour of Woburn to their farmhouse near Newmarket, take friends off for a day at Newmarket races, then home to dinner at the farm. Everyone's ravenous after a day in the open, so what do they get? "Nursery food," says Henrietta Tavistock, "only slightly better. As long as it's nicely cooked and beautifully presented, I think most people enjoy it. Typical dinner after a day at the races? Moussaka, very carefully made, and a huge salad — we always have perfect hedges of lettuce and spinach sprouting away at the farm, and the more you cut them, the more they seem to grow. Then a nice gungey pudding: everyone loves butterscotch pancakes. You can make the pancakes hours beforehand, and simply leave them stacked between pieces of grease-proof paper. Then you make a butterscotch sauce with butter and brown sugar, and as much brandy as possible. The most filthy old brandy will do, but the more the merrier. Then you pour the sauce over the pancakes and put them to warm in the oven."

And nobody minds cheap and cheerful pasta as a main course these days — not if its as special and good as Twiggy's. "I'm not the greatest cook in the world," disclaims Twiggy modestly, "and I can't do a complicated dinner — I'd get in such a state if I had to cook lots of things. So we start with something very simple which I don't have to cook, like avocadoes, then I produce my spaghetti with clams. My boyfriend taught me how to make it in California, where the seafood's really good, and I made it with fresh clams there, but it's still terrific even if you only use those little tins of clams. You can do the sauce in advance too, and then heat it up at the last minute — it thickens up beautifully, so all you have to worry about is cooking the spaghetti. For my clam sauce, I chop lots of onions and lots of garlic and melt them in oil, then I skin and chop masses of tomatoes and add that, then I drain off the juice from the tin of clams, and add them, and season. Lovely. Oh, and a huge big salad — my favourite is made from raw spinach with lots of chopped fennel and vinaigrette dressing.

Starters:

At Robert Carrier's posh restaurant in Camden Town, there's one starter so unendingly popular they're never allowed to take it off the menu: a perfect cucumber salad. "Terribly simple and terribly cheap," explains Robert. "You peel and slice the cucumbers paper-thin, then you put them straight into a little vinaigrette dressing with fresh tarragon and leave it to chill for an hour. Then you drain off the dressing — into which the cumcumber will have shed all its own bitter juice — and put it into more vinaigrette dressing with more tarragon — or fresh chives, or parsley — and chill it again. At the last minute, you add a dollop of slightly salted whipped cream. The combination of the fresh herby taste and the bland cream is delicious."

Home-made fishy patés, served with wedges of lemon and plenty of hot toast, are another low-priced starter, particularly if you have the marvellous Moulinex Moulinette to do the hard work for you. Use smoked mackerel or kipper fillets from which you have stripped the skin and lovingly gleaned every possible bone — yes, a VERY fiddly job — throw in half its weight in butter, a spot of lemon juice, a dash of cayenne pepper, and blend it into a rough paté. Everyone always loves it.

Attention to detail and presentation are half the battle in Nouveau Poor entertaining. Serve perfect melba toast with your patés, for instance, made in Caroline Conran's foolproof way. She toasts slices of bread, slices them through the middle, then toasts the untoasted side under the grill. They can then be served at once — thin, delicious, slightly curled — or done in advance and heated up later. And if the French loaf you bought in a rush turns out to be all leathery and stale, here's another Conran trick. Give it a good steam at the spout of your kettle, then pop it in a hot oven for five minutes. Miraculous. Better still, if you know how, produce home-made bread and say so. People are more impressed by home-made bread than any other single culinary achievement.

Some starters are so obvious it never occurs to anyone to serve them. Like plain classic egg mayonnaise, for instance, made with proper home-made mayonnaise, and dusted with chopped parsley or paprika. (If you're terrified of making mayonnaise, copy a friend who says it's never gone wrong on her since she bought a plastic baby-bottle, enlarged the hole in the teat, and used it for the tricky oil-pouring bit.) And since the home-made kind of mayonnaise tends to come out delightfully thick and wodgy, you can both thin and stretch it by adding boiling water a coffeespoonful at a time.

For hungrier diners, a more solid starter is pancakes with spinach and cheese sauce. Both the pancakes and the spinach can be got ready the day before, if necessary. Make a stack of small pancakes, have ready plenty of cheese sauce and some puréed spinach. Build up a sort of layer cake of pancake, spinach and cheese sauce, repeated over and over until you've used up all the pancakes and spinach, top it

with plenty of cheese sauce, and put it into a hot oven for ten minutes to heat through. Pancakes are not only one of the simplest but also one of the cheapest and more versatile of ideas for impoverished cooks. You could star them as a main course too, stuffed with a creamy mix of chicken and mushrooms, and covered with more cheese sauce.

Main Course:

Who can afford to serve large helpings of expensive meat these days? And even if we could... "I think it's vulgar now to serve up huge lumps of roast beef; in these times, it's unnecessary," says Hardy Amies severely — and he's a man who enjoys good food as much as anyone we know. So it's back to what were once laughingly known as the Cheaper Cuts of Meat, or else that unfailing pauper's standby, chicken.

Top of the Cheap Cuts' league is, of course, lamb, with which you can make nursery-food favourites like Irish Stew and Lancashire Hot Pot — dishes once thought too humble to appear at grand dinner-parties, but who gives grand dinner-parties now?

In early summer, when lamb is at its cheapest and young vegetables are no longer an extravagance, you can serve it as a delicate Navarin, carefully made with fresh young peas and carrots and new potatoes. For winter, lamb makes a more robust stew, pieces of best end and scrag or breast rolled in seasoned flour and fried in dripping with lots of onions, then added to stock with carrots and garlic and potatoes and simmered very slowly for a couple of hours. Any lamb stew is twice as good made the day before, then heated through slowly — which gives you a chance to skin off some of that excess white fat on the top. And even the cheapest of stews looks marvellous presented with lots of freshly chopped parsley on top, and accompanied by hot crisp bread or rolls.

More cheapish lamb: those little baby joints consisting of best end of neck cutlets, trimmed and chined by your butcher. Roast them fairly quickly in a hot oven, basting them with a little stock; keep them nicely pink; and serve them with a huge sinful Gratin Dauphinois — slices of potato swimming in cream and butter.

The trickiest way to serve chicken for a dinner party is also the most expensive — in other words, plain roast. Unless one of you is a fast and masterly carver, everybody ends up with hacked bits of chicken, it's cold in a minute, and there never seems to be quite enough. So every entertaining cook's repertoire should include at least one slightly off beat made-up chicken dish, to be served with rice or noodles. One of our favourites is Margaret Costa's Chicken Pilaff, from her *Four Seasons Cookery Book:* a delicately spiced combination of chicken, onions and almonds with a touch of cinnamon, which follows nicely on the heels of a fish paté.

Although to some people no meal is complete without a salad, just as many people never seem to touch it at all, so it's a great waste to produce a large elaborate salad. Keep it small and simple, chilly and tart, as a palate-cleanser before pudding: plain lettuce or chicory, with plenty of mustard stirred into the vinaigrette dressing, and lots of parsley scattered over the top. (One way and another, no Nouveau Poor cook can afford to be without ample supplies of parsley. You do grow your own, don't you?)

Puddings

There was a time when everybody was presumed to be on a permanent diet, and no nice hostess served puddings. Instead she laid on vast quantities of fresh fruit and assorted French cheeses. No nice hostess *doesn't* serve a pudding these days. We should all feel cruelly robbed if there isn't one, and the cost of serving little assortments of French cheeses, which always get wastefully left, has gone through the roof. So forget about fruit, buy one superb chunk of a good English cheese (which always gets eaten up), and concentrate on a cheap and lovely pudding.

Three of the cheapest are also three of the most wildly successful when properly made — Apple Charlotte, Bread and Butter Pudding, and Apple Crumble. Hardened city tycoons, transported straight back to the nursery, have been known to break down with sheer nostalgic pleasure; and if you're specially broke, you don't have to serve cream as well. Chocolate mousse, ridiculously easy to make, is another sure thing. And if you pick the soft fruit in season, you can serve lots of it stewed and hot, together with Poor Man's Crême Brulée — rice cooked with plenty of milk and a little sugar, then chilled, into which you stir fresh orange juice and a little cream; then glaze the top by coating it with sugar and popping it under the grill before chilling again.

Awful Warning: having cooked and served up perfect food — forget it. One hostess we know has a maddening habit of breaking into interesting political discussions to exclaim worriedly, "I knew it — too much salt," so that her guests have to drop everything to reassure her. If the food is a success your guests will probably say so, and if it's a flop, the less anybody is compelled to discuss it the better. Hostesses who curl the lip at eager smokers-between-courses, or chivy everyone away from the cosy talkative table to drink coffee elsewhere, aren't our idea of bliss either.

LARGE WEEKEND LUNCH PARTIES

This sort of party is immensely popular with everybody, and most people are so delighted to be gathered together in this warm friendly way that all they ask is lots of plonk, and something cheap and tasty for it to wash down. Katharine White-horn has just discovered how to make cannelloni. "Or rather Mennucci have: we feed every-body on simply vast quantities of them. I stuff them with a mixture of cheap smoked collar bacon, mushroom stalks, bread, lots of onions, herbs, all put through the mincer; then I put them in a flattish dish, and cover them with lots of sloshy tomato (a tinful of those smashed up ones will do) and cover it all over with plenty of cheese sauce. A sharp green salad, lots of bread and cheese and that's it."

For more refined eating — and warmer weather — cold chicken in curried mayonnaise is interestingly exotic, and if you serve an enormous cold rice salad with it, an extremely cheap way to feed large numbers of people. Home-made mayonnaise is obviously nicest, and you can make it with groundnut or sunflower oil rather than the best olive oil. Into this, you dump a dollop of curry powder, a little red wine, a spot of lemon juice, a spoonful of apricot jam, paprika and cayenne to taste, ditto salt and pepper, a dash of Worcester sauce, a dash of tabasco, and a spot of tomato purée, and stir it all up together before ladling it over all the little bits of chicken. The great trick of a cold rice salad, we learned from Elizabeth David, is lots of freshly grated nutmeg and freshly ground black pepper, stirred in while the rice is still hot, together with the olive oil; after that it's over to you — lemon, nuts, raisins, chunks of tomato, cubes of cucumber or whatever, according to your fancy.

A friend of ours once produced a fantastic three-course banquet for about twenty people — and admitted afterwards that the food had cost her less than fifty pence a head. Her lunch began with herbed garlic bread — hot french loaves stuffed with butter and herbs as well as crushed garlic, served with a big goulash with potatoes, and coleslaw made with home-made mayonnaise. Meringues filled with ginger cream, served with slices of fresh pineapple were the glorious finale, and nobody moved for at least an hour. "Easy really," she explained airily. "I bought a great big white cabbage, terribly cheap; eggs were cheap at the time, too, so I made mayonnaise with lots of egg yolks, then used up the whites to make meringues. And they were practically giving away pineapples that week."

HUGE EVENING PARTIES

Huge evening parties for forty to fifty people simply can't be too dressy. When girl-friends ask you what to wear, tell them the prettiest dress they own, and look a knock-out yourself — nothing gets a party off to a better start. Unless it's midsummer, dowse most of the lights and put candles, candles everywhere. Women guests will love you for it. Parties like this are the easiest kind to cater for. As Elizabeth David so rightly says, "The main thing is for the hostess not to wear herself out for days beforehand, fussing about with aspic, making patterns with mayonnaise and sticking little things on sticks..." And guests at this kind of party are usually so grateful to you for undertaking to feed such numbers at all that they couldn't be less critical. (It's kind, though, to make it clear whether there's food or not: nothing is more irritating than being invited for that noncommittal hour nine pm and stuffing down a couple of sandwiches beforehand, only to find on arrival that the boards are groaning with food.)

It's worse than pointless to have complicated food that needs concentration, balance and both hands; what's perfect is something hot, tasty, substantial and not too runny, that can be managed off one big plate with a fork. Have a choice of two sharp salads people can put on their plates at the same time — perhaps lettuce, and fresh tomato with onions and chives; and have plenty of piping hot bread and plenty of butter. Don't bother with quantities of cheese and fruit: having prised themselves out of their cosy chats to collect food, people are always reluctant to move again once they've settled down unless they're actually starving. You could, though, carry round bowls of a yummy cold sweet later on: a tipsy home-made trifle; chilled puréed apple (apples you've baked in their skins and then put through the Mouli) into which you've stirred a dash of cream, lemon juice and sugar; a tangy fruit mousse; all accompanied by tiny sweet biscuits, which you can make yourself for small cost and effort.

For feeding vast numbers, what's actually cheap? "Rice, really is the only possibility," says dishy cookery writer Fanny Ward. "And you can't even call that cheap any more. I use brown Riceland rice, and I make huge risottoes, into which I throw bits of chicken, walnuts, garlic, chopped liver, almost anything really, especially if it's a good bright colour. If the room's fairly dark, nobody really notices what they're eating — especially with all that noise and chat and drinking going on."

Chicken or lamb are, once more, the best meat to put into

this kind of risotto or pilaff — padded with huge quantities of onions, tomatoes, garlic, herbs, raisins or nuts.

Designer Thea Porter gives lovely parties in her beautiful Mayfair flat — she once asked all her guests to come dressed in black and white — and serves deliciously exotic food. "I do love giving parties," says Thea, "and it's such hell these days to have to stop and think all the time whether you can possibly afford to entertain your friends. But my great discovery is the marvellous Chinese supermarkets — there's one just off Shaftesbury Avenue — everything is so much cheaper there. They sell those little mange-tout peas, ginger, and the best curry-paste I know — it's called Lekari and it comes mild or hot. When I'm feeling broke, I make very simple cheap curries, with lots of little side dishes — I use plenty of onions and tomatoes and a spot of ginger. Crab makes a delicious curry, too. Crab is so cheap — you can get three enormous ones for about one pound fifty pence. And in the Chinese supermarkets they sell huge packets of frozen crab for just over one pound."

A great dish for large-party entertaining suggested by Robert Carrier is his Creole Jambalaya, from *Great Dishes of the World*. "It sounds terribly extravagant because of all those shrimps," Robert explains, "but you can perfectly well leave them out and put in extra ham instead. And you can stretch it with lots more rice to feed great numbers."

One advantage of parties with buffet food, from the guest's point of view, is that it gives everyone a heaven-sent excuse to detach themselves from a conversation, so apart from looking after lame ducks, there's absolutely no excuse for hostesses to rush round officiously crying "Circulate" to happy little groups of chat.

And our awful warning is for those who fail to provide strong black coffee at some point after food. Serve it in horrid paper cups or chipped mugs, make it from Camp or the lowest grade of Instant, give guests no more than an inch, and fail to supply them with sugar: they'll forgive you. But leave them coffeeless altogether, and you'll have ruined the evening for a good fifty per cent of your guests.

N.B. Some of us can't tell Nescafé Continental made double strength from freshly-made coffee, either.

THE DISCO PARTY

Finally, for the young and energetic, featuring food, drink and plenty of loud music for dancing. The music won't be your problem, generally speaking, but the food and drink will. The food should be hearty, plentiful, delicious and simple: a pasta situation if ever there was one. Serve cannelloni, spaghetti or lasagne, with plenty of grated cheese, piping hot French bread and butter, and a salad for those who want it. Have a supply of cheese for anyone with a giant appetite, and serve one delicious pudding — a fresh fruit salad takes a lot of beating, we think, made with bananas, oranges, lots of whatever fruit is in season, and lots of orange juice for the liquid.

BOOZE

The skeleton at any feast these days is the horrific price of booze. There's no such thing as cheap wine any more, even beer is getting to be a bit of a luxury, and the good old days when hosts could afford to offer gin and tonic before, good claret during dinner and brandy or whisky after, have disappeared for ever as far as we can see. There are, however, ways in which to cut the cost of boozing without spoiling the party.

Wine

If you're serving straight plonk out of those huge two-litre bottles, decant it into the cheapest, plainest glass decanters you can find. And serve it in ordinary wine-glasses if possible (some wine-merchants hire them out for a purely nominal fee) not huge tumblers. Otherwise your guests will swill it like beer; the mere sight of a two-litre bottle has this effect on a lot of us.

Two-litre bargains aren't necessarily the cheapest form of wine, either. It's well worth cultivating your local wine-merchant who will probably be able to point you to much better value in ordinary-sized bottles from time to time. Probably the best

solution to the problem is to buy wine at auctions, when you'll pick up good French wines for about a pound a bottle if you set about it the right way. Daria and Alexander Schouvaloff buy all their wines in this way.

"Keep away from the good auctions; what you want are the sales of inexpensive wines — usually there's about one a month in London," Daria advises. "You have to go to the tasting beforehand — it's usually in the morning. You walk around, sample, work out prices. Start with the sherries, then the white wine, then the red. If you start with the red, your palate is destroyed. Its very important to listen. The real dealers are walking around saying things like "I think I'll try a couple of dozen cases of this one," and if you're a woman, they never pay any attention to you quietly eavesdropping. The chat is invaluable. You have to work out, too, what you're going to bid — write down the auctioneer's estimates (they're always written up on a big list) next to the the lots you're interested in in your catalogue. And don't forget to add VAT at eight per cent a case. Two rules: don't get drunk before you start bidding. Seriously! And never join in the first bid for any lot. Whoever gets it has an option on all the cases in it, so you risk losing it, but the price usually goes down over the next few cases."

If you really can't afford to serve even the vilest plonk, how about making your own? Lots of people do, and they always swear its as good as the best French, though their friends don't always agree. It's not an enterprise to be embarked on lightly, though, as Jonathan Gathorne-Hardy made plain to us.

"I made my own wine for about two years, then I gave it up because I found I was simply permanently drunk. I used to make it in vast quantities — two great twelve-gallon demi-johns all bubbling away, and sometimes there would be as many as 150 bottles in the rack. It's perfectly simple really but basically you have to allow at least twenty pounds for initial outlay — bottles and airlocks and so on — and about six months before you're really in business.

"I did it just like they tell you in all those books, and I was producing perfectly drinkable stuff — comparable, say, with a pounds worth of plonk from Oddbins — for about twenty pence a bottle. My friends didn't seem to notice they were drinking anything particularly out of the way — the trick is to serve it in unlabelled bottles, and not go on about it all the time.

"I used to go to a terribly good place in Soho, where they sell the grape juice in much larger quantities than you can usually buy, but in Boots they're always very good too, rather like an old-fashioned ironmonger, and they'll advise you on tricky problems. Space? You need somewhere you can keep at an even 70°. I just happened to have a small coal-cellar, and I used a greenhouse heater. The first two or three lots I made came out fairly disgusting, but even then, I found that when I mixed them

half and half with the cheapest shop-bought plonk I could find, they seemed perfectly drinkable and not too revolting. I found the white came out best in the end. And it definitely gets better if you leave it.

"There are two dangers. In the first place, if it doesn't ferment enough before you bottle it, the bottles simply explode their corks out — fearful waste and frightful mess. And then however carefully you filter it, you always seem to leave a lot of the impurities in — and the hangovers are absolutely appalling. I might have got better at that if I'd gone on, I suppose."

Beer

If wine is fraught with peril, though, home-brewing your own beer is child's play, according to thriller-writer Gavin Lyall:

"I've been making my own for a year now — I make a bitter and a lager. Its very simple indeed, and it worked perfectly well the first time. I simply bought one of those Boots kits which have everything in them, and a five-gallon plastic bucket, and that was more or less that as far as equipment goes. The biggest initial investment is also the nicest — you need lots and lots of empty beer bottles... After that there are various little bits and pieces to be bought from time to time — sugar, sterilising tablets to make sure that everything is perfectly clean and so on. But basically, it works out at about five pence a pint, and if I say it myself, it's not bad at all. Not as good as the best ale, of course, but it compares perfectly well with the lager or bitter you get in most pubs."

As Gavin's wife, Katherine Whitehorn says, "If you offer people a gin and tonic on Sunday morning they'll always say yes, but we find that quite a lot of men are just as happy — if not happier — with beer."

Aperitifs

In fact we can all forget about gin and tonic — even tonic is ruinous these days. Serve the classic aperitifs instead — Chambery vermouth, well chilled, or a light dry sherry. When Shirley Conran was flat broke between jobs, she used to keep a bottle of Amontillado sherry — that dark sweetish one — to offer people: "It's a perfectly respectable drink to offer, but as nobody actually likes it, a little of it goes a long way".

After dinner

For those expensive guests who, once seated at the dinner-table basically want to keep on drinking till they go home, a small glass of port is a very grand substitute for the once-obligatory brandy. After, or in-stead of that, a chilled medium white wine makes pleasant after-dinner boozing. And we love the civilised French habit of producing chilly fruit juice about an hour after dinner. Its much cheaper than brandy, and most people like it even better.

Teenage parties

As far as the younger generation is concerned, don't produce a virtually non-alcoholic fruit cup and think you're combining thrift with wisdom — you're simply getting your children a reputation for being lousy hosts. Children have as strong a resistance as any adult to those suspicious-looking mixtures full of soggy bits of fruit and veg. Serve Lord Byron's favourite drink instead — hock and seltzer: in other words, white wine to which you add equal parts of soda to produce a delicious, fresh and festive drink. Or else a youthful version of Vin Blanc Cassis — white wine with a splash of soda and a dash of Ribena. (But for heaven's sake, empty the bottle into an elegant decanter.)

Eating Ethnic

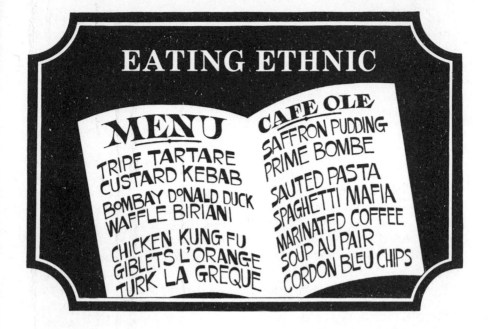

EATING ETHNIC

MENU

TRIPE TARTARE
CUSTARD KEBAB
BOMBAY DONALD DUCK
WAFFLE BIRIANI

CHICKEN KUNG FU
GIBLETS L'ORANGE
TURK LA GRECQUE

CAFE OLE

SAFFRON PUDDING
PRIME BOMBE

SAUTED PASTA
SPAGHETTI MAFIA
MARINATED COFFEE
SOUP AU PAIR
CORDON BLEU CHIPS

Who owns the chocolate coloured Rolls and the midnight blue Mercedes, nightly jostling each other on the double yellow lines outside the grander restaurants? They can't all be Arabs, can they?

Certainly it's nobody we know because our friends can't afford to eat at this sort of restaurant any more. It's not *just* the choking over the vinaigrette when you're being charged £1.75 for a 20p. artichoke. It is also the growing feeling that no hot dinner, however exquisitely and lovingly prepared, is worth £12.

So, we're eating ethnic instead, at a quarter the cost. These days there is hardly a High Street or back street that doesn't contain an Indian or Chinese restaurant or a kebab place. And the food is nicer than you'll find in one of those staid, ''warmed-up-meat-and-two-veg'' provincial hotels or in any of the plush

restaurants that charge a great deal for scampi, steak and fruit salad (''Fresh? Oh no, madam. I don't *think* so!''). Anyway, if you're trying to eat anywhere outside the very centre of a big town after nine o'clock, you'll be spared any choice in the matter since the Oriental restaurants will be the only ones still serving food.

INDIAN RESTAURANTS

The problem for most of us, when we eat Indian or Chinese, is how to avoid collecting an embarrassing plethora of plates, all of them, apparently, containing either fried noodles or fried rice.

How, in fact, to order?

Slap, bang in the middle of London's Chinatown, in Gerrard Street, there is, rather surprisingly, an Indian restaurant called The Ganges. The proprietors, Mr and Mrs Ahmed, are helpful folk. They will give any diner, who asks for it, a free leaflet of their excellent recipes and they have thoughtfully devised a kind of master plan for finding your way around an Indian menu. It goes something like this:

Starter: one portion, per person, from any of the following: fish, meat or chicken dish, grill, kebab or Tandoori dish, soup or fish cocktail, a dish of Samosas. (Samosas are triangular shaped pastry savouries, full of spicy minced meat).

Second course: one portion, per person, from a cereal group (could be rice or Pulao rice or one of the three kinds of bread on offer here — Tandoori Nan, Tandoori Roti or Paratha); one portion each of a Curry, Tandoori or Kebab; a half portion each of a vegetable or Dal side dish. Chutney.

Third Course: choose from one of the almond flavoured sweets, fruits or yogurt.

The way to get bowl after bowl of rice is to order, say, a Prawn Pulao and a Chicken Biryani and a dish of fried rice on the side. It's probably lack of communication, rather than sadism, which makes the Indian waiter nod and smile politely when you ask diffidently, "Don't you think we'd better have an extra dish of rice?" In fact Pulaos are based on rice and Biryanis are a complete meal containing rice, curry and some vegetables. It's also possible to get your side plate piled up with various kinds of bread if you order a nan or a paratha *and* a papadom. Papadoms are wafer thin, and nans and parathas are plump and moist and fattening and delicious. Of course you don't need to go through the three-course marathon. A combination of dishes from the second course or a single Biryani make a satisfying meal.

Useful words to jot on a cuff:

Tandoori means that the food has been marinaded in herbs and cooked in a huge, clay jar with slow burning charcoal in the base. These clay pots are also used for cooking the Tandoori bread. Tandoori food is crisp on the outside, succulent inside and if it is dry then your Indian restaurant either hasn't got a proper Tandoori pot or they have been doing too much pre-cooking.

Tikka indicates that the meat has been taken off the bone, spiced, possibly marinaded in yogurt and then grilled on charcoal.

Vindaloo curry is very hot, Madras and Korma are not quite so hot and Dhansak is hot, sweet and sour and there are probably lentils about.

Dal is a pureed lentil dish, seasoned with herbs and spices, Sag means spinach and Bhindi or Okra are those pretty, green 'ladies fingers' you often see in street markets and wonder how to cook. Answer: swiftly and lightly with as little water as possible and a dot of butter. Like cabbage, they must not be mushy.

One of the economic joys of taking somebody out to an Indian meal is that you don't have to order wine and can get away with draughts of lager or a jug of lassee, a chilled, lemon-tangy yogurt drink. Contrary to general belief, wine does taste lovely with Indian food, providing you choose a fruity white or rosé.

Southern Indian restaurants are just beginning to happen in England. You can spot them by the vegetarian slant to the menu. Here you'll find dishes like Iddaly (small, steamed patties made from ground dried peas and coarsely ground rice and served with a mouth-searingly hot lentil sauce) and Dosais.

Humphrey Lyttleton is very fond of Dosais. He's given up eating for *Harpers & Queen* magazine because, he says, after so many years as a food writer he can hardly stand the sight of food any longer. But, he still goes along to The Vijay in Willesden Lane, N.W.6. for a Masala Dosai: "Dosais are large, crisp, rice-flour pancakes with various fillings. The Masala has a potato filling which sounds terribly boring, but it has a wonderful, herby flavour. They serve it at The Vijay with a side dish of coconut and it's very cheap. Well, it must be cheap because lots of musicians can afford to eat there."

Larry Adler (there must be some sort of affinity between musicians and food) has now taken over Humphrey Lyttleton's column in *Harpers & Queen* and says he's upset that you can't get his favourite ethnic food, properly prepared, in England: "Hot pastrami on rye. It's a Jewish delicacy, spiced beef sliced very, very thin. Absolutely marvellous. In Beverley Hills, recently, I saw a queue of two hundred people at nine o'clock in the morning, all waiting outside Nate 'n' Al's for their hot pastrami. Naturally, I joined the queue and it *almost* made me consider going back to live in the States."

CHINESE COOKING

"The next best ethnic dish to Pastrami," says Larry Adler, "is the Seecheune Rice I had at Wat's House in Allitsen Road, St Johns Wood, the other day. Prawns sauteed with hot green chillies and served on rice. As good as anything I've eaten in Hong Kong."

Quentin Crewe knows more about eating out than anyone else in the country and now writes a restaurant column for *Vogue*: "The thing about eating cheaply is that it should look pretty and be fun. Dim Sum are tiny, light dumpling with lots of different fillings and they arrive at the table piled up in a little wooden sieves. Eat one layer, lift off the sieve and there's more deliciousness underneath. They look like ravioli, but are much nicer. Dim Sum go right through Oriental cuisine. I've had them at The Lido in Gerrard Street and they are also very good at the Siam Restaurant in St Albans Grove, Kensington. The only disadvantage is that they are a lunch-time dish and come off the menu at six o'clock, because they are meant to be a tea-time snack."

We had Dim Sum at the Chuen-Cheng-Ku in Wardour Street (where, incidentally, *Evening Standard* writer Fay Maschler recommends the Crab in Black Bean Sauce) with Kenneth Lo. Mr Lo is a world authority on Chinese cuisine and has written fourteen books on the subject.

He says we needn't feel diffident about ordering different kinds of food together because that's the way the Chinese eat, too. "It's important to get a contrast of colour, texture and taste — as in any meal. For instance, for two people, Char Siu Pork or Duck (Char Siu means it's barbecued) on rice, a dish of beef on rice (or some steamed fish instead) and an accompanying dish of vegetables would be a good selection."

Most Chinese restaurants serve either Cantonese food or bastard Cantonese, tailored to the English Taste. Cantonese cooking is very savoury, the strong ingredients producing an immediate explosion of tastes in the mouth, cleverly concealing the fact that half a pound of meat is stretching to feed six people. Peking cooking is plainer, simpler, there is more meat, an abundance of giant prawns and the flavours are more usually added with sauces and condiments at the table. Mr Lo recommends a Peking dinner when there are half a dozen or more people eating together so you can enjoy a Mongolian Hotpot. A huge bowl of steaming broth is placed in the centre of the table, you throw in the meat and vegetables, leave them a few minutes and then retrieve them à la fondu, drinking the delicate soup as a finale. Peking Duck, the other popular Pekinese delicacy is crispy, succulent duck rolled up in thin pancakes with spring onions, cucumber and a soya based sauce. One of the best dishes in the world.

If you're ordering for two in an ordinary High-Street Chinese restaurant Mr Lo suggests a portion of fried rice, some spare ribs ("English people love them!"), a dish of quick fry beef in oyster sauce and a portion of bean sprouts.

The cunning of these last two dishes is that they have to be cooked to order: "Never order mixed vegetables as they may be pre-cooked and soggy." Mr Lo thinks that Chow Mein (a composite dish of noodles, vegetables and meat) is the best bet if you are eating alone and refuses to be snobby about Chop Suey: "People say it's not *really* Chinese," he says. "Well, maybe it isn't but it is certainly just about the only real ethnic dish in America. Chop Suey is the Chinese word for 'hash' and Chinese labourers prepared it for the Irish when they arrived in San Francisco with the railroad. A sort of Chinese-Irish stew!"

Tea is the perfect accompaniment to Chinese food and, if you're nervous of chopsticks, just watch the way the Chinese use them. They don't do a polite British balance from table to mouth. They hold the bowl right under their chins and shovel the food in.

Sue Miles, who writes for *Time Out,* speaks glowingly of Chinese wind-dried meat. This is evidently a connoisseur's delight, since the walls of the restaurant where we choked over this dish are festooned with glowing accolades from sundry food writers. We felt you might as well tuck into a plate of salted leather and were *much* happier with Sue's other ethnic suggestion, which was Meze.

GREEK, GREEK-CYPRIOT AND TURKISH-CYPRIOT RESTAURANTS

They all serve Meze as a sort of hors d'oeuvre. One Meze is more than enough for two people and we were greedily wiping our pitta (Greek bread) around half a dozen or so bowls of goodies at Nontas in Camden High Street, when the waiter came over and murmured that this was just the starter to the starter, as it were. The Meze continued with lamb stew, kebabs, rice and salad. A feast for less than £2.

The two most popular first courses in Greek restaurants are Taramasalata, a delicious cod's roe pató, and Humus, which is a purée of chick peas and oil. If there are two of you eating, order one each and dip your pitta into both dishes. Talatouri (yogurt and cucumber) could be a starter or a side dish with Kebabs. Kebabs are usually made with lamb or pork and served on rice with a lot of raw onion. Sheftalia is a spiced minced meat kebab and usually a bit cheaper. The thing that tends to make delicious Greek meals so extraordinarily low priced is that you nearly always get the rice and the salad (mixed, with olives and Feta — a goat cheese) and the pitta thrown in with the cost of the kebab.

Other Greek dishes you'll find on the menu are Moussaka, an up-market shepherds pie with aubergines and a savoury custard topping, Dolmades which are mince-stuffed vine leaves and Afelia, chunks of pork in wine. Greek restaurants are great for festive occasions because the waiters are inclined to break into jolly song, or strum a bouzouki or grab sympathetic-looking diners into a conga-line for Zorba's dance. They also have a disturbing habit, for Nouveau Poor diners, which is to throw the plates into a crashing pile in the centre of the room. Small children love this wasteful ethnic tradition.

Turkish Cypriots are now opening restaurants all over the place and we've even seen Turkish Doner Kebab stalls in the street. A Doner Kebab is a large piece of spiced and filleted lamb wrapped around a giant skewer which revolves in front of a fire. Slices are cut off and served with salad and pitta. A kebab and salad, dropped into a hot pitta, makes perfect take-away food and we reckon that Doner Kebab Take-Aways (being cheaper than ordinary kebabs) are going to replace Colonel Sanders and his Kentucky Fried Chicken as the modern child's alternative to Mum's cooking. Aside from the Doner, Turkish Cypriot food in England is much the same as the Greek, and both serve lovely sticky Baklava, a mouth-watering mixture of flaky pastry, honey and nuts.

What to drink with Greek and Turkish food? Turkish red wines all seem to be reasonably priced and mellow, but the ideal compliment to spicy kebabs is a Greek white wine called Retsina which tastes rather as though the pips and bark have gone into the bottle along with the grapes. Some people can't drink it without getting massively hung over. Thick Turkish coffee can be too sweet and thick for English palates, so play safe and ask for the medium strength.

ITALIAN TRATTORIAS

Italian Trattorias aren't such a bargain as they used to be, since many of them have become very grand and now won't let you get away with *just* a dish of pasta and a salad in the evening or during the lunch-hour rush. But the Spaghetti Houses give good value and don't insist on their customers ordering two or three courses. (Though we were rather surprised to see the pictures of Heinz tins stocked up to the ceiling of the cellar under the Knightsbridge branch during that horrific siege.)

Besides the obvious Spaghetti Bolognese (meat sauce) and Milanaise (tomato sauce), there's also Vongole (shellfish and masses of garlic) and Carbonara, where raw eggs are scrambled by tossing them into the hot spaghetti. Lasagne and Canneloni taste much the same, the main difference being that one is made with layers of flat pasta and the other with stuffed rolls of pasta, and Pizzas are cheap and filling and don't taste very nice unless they have been freshly made the same day.

Trattorias are the place to take children for special treats because all children love pasta and all Italian waiters love children. Indeed, it's rather vexing to sit with your loved one in a glamourous, candle-lit Apicella setting and have all the staff's attentions concentrated on a moppet of six at the next table. As journalist Sally Vincent once remarked, after watching a tiny diner at one of Mario and Franco's places having her cushion adjusted and her cheeks tweaked: "If there are lollipops going *I* want one, too!"

When Fay Maschler tried out as many cafés, pubs and wine bars as she could stand, to find the best cheap lunch in London, she came out in favour of the little English-type 'caffs' run by old-established Italian families. This sort of Italian food is still cheap — you can get good home-made minestrone, a meat dish and a coffee for around £1 a head — but the setting isn't very glamorous.

AMERICAN FOOD

American ethnic eating may mean Chop Suey to a Chinese but to the rest of us it's surely hamburgers? American hamburgers are meatier and far superior to the English variety and their salads are usually good and crisp and there's a great selection of horrid dressings. MacDonalds, the huge American chain, are now establishing themselves over here and, if the fare is unexcitingly tasteless, at least the service is swift and the surroundings wholesomely hygienic. The Hard Rock Cafe in Old Park Lane, W.1, is still the best value in hamburger joints because the disco-loud music makes for an electric atmosphere. The place to take the kids when they have outgrown Italian waiters.

There are plenty more ethnic restaurants around but they aren't cheap. The **Germans, Austrians** and **Czechs** all like sauerkraut, stews with dumplings and cheesecakes and you get a lot of it for your money. **Japanese** food seems to include a great deal of raw fish wrapped in seaweed and if you go to a really authentic Japanese restaurant you could find yourself sitting, cross-legged, on the floor and cooking your own food in a pot over a dear little hot-plate. Personally, we'd rather do the cooking at home and eat it in comfort. The best **Spanish** dishes, like Paella, are a mix of fish and rice and Gazpacho (iced tomato soup) is a superb summer starter. The **Danes** are dotty about open-sandwiches, and a slice of rye topped with smoked eel, mayonnaise and a gherkin, plus a cup of coffee, at the Danish Centre in Conduit Street, W.1., can cost as much as a three course meal in a simple cafe.

FRENCH RESTAURANTS

They are no place for the Nouveau Poor, unless you've got the nerve and style of a friend of ours who, sitting in one of the grandest restaurants in St Tropez, was handed the menu and suddenly realised he couldn't afford a thing on it: "Pommes-frites all round..." he said. "And some water, if you please."

ENGLISH FOOD

Pubs are ethnic British and most of them do seem to share the English disinterest in good food. Shepherds pie cut into square, livid-orange wedges, over-cooked beef salads, ready-made pork pies, and did ploughmen *really* survive on those tiny slices of cheese and an inch of foil wrapped butter? There's nothing nicer than home-cooked food served with a pint of draught bitter in the convivial atmosphere of an old English pub, but it hardly ever happens outside a television ad. When it does, the pub is so crowded there's nowhere to sit and the home-cooking comes attached to three-star prices. On the whole, wine bars offer better food and value but with all that delicious wine about it's tempting to order a bottle rather than a single glass of Muscadet...and another.

Fish and Chips is real British ethnic nosh but with the price of the two basic ingredients rising almost daily, you must expect to pay upwards of £1 for the fish alone at a really first-class sit-down fish and chip shop like Geales in Farmer Street, Notting Hill Gate. Fish is so pricey that it's not surprising that most shops are now Frying Tonight chicken or saveloys or scampi or, as in a shop down our way, Frogs Legs and Chips. Anyway, it's not much of a cook's night out treat, to eat your dinner, on the move, out of last week's local paper. Especially when you can enjoy a curry, in a candle-lit restaurant, for the same price.

And, don't believe all those stories about the Indian cuisine being based on Kit-e-Kat. We checked with the people at Westminster City Council who inspect restaurants in the Soho area and none of them could remember a prosecution ever being brought for this reason. Mind you, they could recall plenty of other hygiene infringements but, as they were quick to point out, these were *not* limited to foreigners *or* to cheap restaurants.

If you're very good, Darling…

IF YOU'RE VERY GOOD, DARLING, Mummy Will Give You A Nice Cardboard Box...

The birth-rate of Great Britain has been dropping steadily for the past few years: in 1975 it was the lowest since mid-Depression, 1933.

The most widely-offered explanation is that children cost money, and that more and more of us have less and less of it. So lots of couples probably panicked, and decided that children are such a huge expense that they simply couldn't afford them.

And up to a point, of course, they're absolutely right. If two can live almost as cheaply as one, four live at least twice as expensively as two, and a lot of the luxury disappears from lives which echo with the patter of little feet.

But need children be such a huge expense?

A good third of the money lavished on them, we think, is money straight down the drain, which doesn't buy anything necessary either to the health or the happiness of your little darlings...

THE NEW-BORN BABY

When it's the unique, marvellous first baby, any normal parent is going to be strongly tempted to rush out and buy everything brand-new for this treasure: a new crib with new hand-embroidered sheets and rabbits appliquéd over the blankets, new little nighties, a legion of fluffy brand-new toys, and spotless new nursery equipment in the newly-decorated nursery. (Well, yes, the deep bloodred of the dining room it used to be would be just a tiny bit unsuitable for a nursery.)

But what couples plunged in the happy euphoria of a first baby simply don't grasp is the incredible speed at which babies grow.

Within months, weeks almost, half of that spanking new stuff will have to be relegated to the store room because it will be too small. The crib will give way to the cot, the pram to the push-chair, the tiny little nighties to the one-piece stretch-suit, the mini-bath balanced on a precarious stand to something much sturdier and three times the size. Like, say, the kitchen sink.

And another minor point is that although this equipment gives you immense gratification, all that your baby actually wants is you, warmth and food, and to hell with appliquéd rabbits.

If you're planning a family of four or five, of course, you can always regard new stuff as an investment; it'll get enough wear to give you a good return on your money.

But if you only plan the modern nuclear family of two children maximum — aren't there better ways to spending the cash?

And if you're trying to cost Operation Baby down to its lowest, here's what you needn't budget for:

New crib, new baby-bath, new play-pen, new carry-cot:

The odds are that you know at least one couple whose children are now rushing unwillingly to school every day, but who haven't yet been able to bring themselves to part with these relics of their children's babyhood. They'll simply love to lend them to you. You can always run up new dotted-muslin drapes for the crib, and give the cot and play-pen a fresh lick of paint (lead-free, please) and a new nursery transfer.

If no such friends present themselves, read the classified ads in your local paper, and the cards outside the nearest stationers, which are usually full of unwanted nursery stuff on offer at absurdly low prices. If you still don't strike lucky, try the notices posted outside your local Child Welfare Clinic, or stick one up yourself.

We said *carry-cot*, incidentally, because no parent in their right minds these days is still going to lash out up to £100 to buy one of these Stately Prams of England, which you can't even dismantle to stow in train, plane or car.

Baby-clothes

Don't bother with fragile little knitted *matinee jackets* and be-ribboned *socks* and ditto *mittens*, and *little bonnets*. These will rain in on you from all sides, from doting aunts and grandparents. The modern baby, after the first couple of long-nightie'd weeks of life, goes straight into practical all-in-one stretch garments, and hardly ever wears all that knitted stuff.

By the same token, don't buy lots of fluffy *shawls;* you'll probably get given at least a couple, and if you don't, you can always use the crib-blankets instead.

Modern young friends will give you smashing romper-suits for the baby in practical bright colours; try and steer older, conservative friends in the same direction — though your first baby is still certain to start life with a cupboard full of darling little white, pink or pale blue embroidered and smocked frocks it may not wear even once.

And while we're on the subject of baby-wear, what about *nappies?*

Ordinary terry ones, of course, unless you want to bankrupt yourself buying loads and loads of disposable ones every week, for months and months to come, at prices that go steadily up, up, up. They're seldom entirely satisfactory at night-time; what is more, if you're ecologically-minded, you won't want to consider disposables on such a vast scale; and unlike terry nappies, you can't save up disposables, pass them on to Baby No. 2, and finally recycle them as useful all-purpose domestic rags.

The horror of nappies has anyway been enormously exaggerated: with modern sweet-smelling nappy-soaks, washing-machines and the launderette round the corner, they're hardly a crushing domestic burden; more of a crashing bore.

When you're buying terry-towelling nappies, incidentally, don't ever buy the cheapest on offer: they'll also be the thinnest, and you may need to use two at a time, which hardly makes them an economy. Buy best-quality Seconds at sale-time instead — Harrington's Gold Seal, for instance. Your baby isn't going to gripe over a piece of imperfect hemming.

Baby-room

Another great way to waste money on babies is by turning the nursery into a baby-room: curtains and delicate pastel wallpapers running over with baby bunnies and twee nursery-style patterns, like baby-talk made visible. What's charming for a tiny month-old baby is going to look pretty silly as ambience for a tough two-year-old toddler, and you'll both have to live with it if you can't afford to change it. Nurseries should be warm, bright, colourful rooms, certainly, but you can get just the same effect — and better, in our view — by using ordinary paint on the walls, and a good well-designed print, in clear appealing colours, for the curtains.

Its equally important to bear in mind that tiny babies turn into energetic vandals with disconcerting speed. Plan accordingly.

Paint the walls with wipe-down paint — not a delicate patterned paper that will be ruined by scribbles of wax crayon.

If you're starting from scratch with a bare wooden floor, sand it — you can hire an efficient sanding machine and cover it with a couple of coats of polyurethane varnish for a smooth non-slippy surface. Polyurethane varnish comes in colours as well as uncoloured — you could pick a cheerful deep green or warm red if you wanted, though a natural woody colour will probably keep everyone happier longer. Scatter a couple of nice soft tumbletwist rugs over the barer-looking bits of the nursery floor: they can be dunked in the washing-machine, or sent to the laundry when they get too grubby.

Any carpet in a nursery is going to take a beating: trampled-in plasticine and chewing-gum, spilled milk and splashed water, and worse, bits of food and other oddments, not to mention pee. (It's the acid in pee that's rotten for carpets: take a tip from the Queen who keeps a soda-syphon handy to neutralise the damage her corgis do to the royal carpets.) So it really isn't

worth while putting down brand-new carpet and suffering every time you look at it. On the other hand, plenty of women find cleaning a carpet vastly preferable to wiping mess off lino, and if you feel that way yourself, you'll do better with off-cuts from your nearest carpet-warehouse, or a big friendly rug picked up cheap in an auction, or something begged from granny. (Grannies quite often have two or three carpets piled on top of each other in their homes: it's the best and cheapest way to store them, that's why).

Don't put delicate pieces of furniture in the nursery, unless you want them ruined by rings from cough medicine, trails of bright-pink nail-polish from that memorable occasion when you accidentally left the bottle in the nursery at siesta-time, crayon and chalk-marks, and ballpoint-pen doodles. Much better to use up — or buy in — old, unspecial

pieces of furniture. Sandpaper any rough or splintery bits firmly off them, give them a couple of coats of fresh bright paint to suit your nursery colour-scheme, and there you are.

Don't waste money on expensive child-pictures or even those pricey posters to hang on the nursery walls: you can buy smashing wrapping-paper these days for around ten or twelve pence a big sheet, which are every bit as good as pictures. We've seen colourful flower-prints, reproductions of samplers, naïve farmyard scenes in a repeat pattern that could be chopped up and used as a frieze, copies of C17 Dutch skating scenes, and plenty more. Pictures for the nursery needn't necessarily be childish: if you see a splendid poster in your local travel agency, ask him nicely if you can have it for your children when he's finished with it.

Later on, when the children are old enough to splash the paint around, you can mount and hang their own efforts. Ask them to paint something specially for the nursery, and to choose the colours themselves.

And if you want to buy your children a particularly special present, why not a small original painting or a good lithograph?

Don't use drawing-pins to fix posters or wrapping-paper pictures to the nursery walls: children tend to yank them down if they're in reach. Instead, use Blue Tack, the Landlady's Friend: a small blob of it holds paper magically in place without marking either it or the surface it clings to. Unbelievable stuff. You can buy it from W.H. Smith and most good stationers.

The Baby-food Bill:

It's a delightful thought that thanks to inflation many thousands of babies are likely to start life breast-fed who would otherwise have been raised on the bottle. In October 1975, *Which* worked out that formula-feeding a baby could cost anything up to £23 for the first eighteen weeks of its life — and milk prices have gone up since then — as opposed to breast-feeding which doesn't cost a bean and is much, much better for a baby.

But money spent on all that powdered milk is just the start. By the time they're three or four months old, most babies are already launched on a regular diet of those little tins and jars. And if you do it the way those charming, helpful babyfood leaflets suggest, you could be opening up and shoving into your infant five or six little jarfuls a day by the time he's six months old, although modern nutritional thinking is that he should only just be *starting* on solids around this age. At about eight pence to ten pence a crack, that's an awful lot of money for a diet of boring tinned food. For just a little more of your time, your baby could be eating delicious, tasty fresh food. And you could be saving, according to the same *Which* report, around £1 a week.

There's nothing specially mysterious about baby diets either: its more a question of a little knowledge and a lot of common sense.

Your baby needs *protein:* so give him tiny quantities of minced meat or chicken, liver, white fish, egg yolk (add the white later, some babies are allergic to it). The liver and egg-yolk are also excellent sources of the *iron* he needs. He needs small amounts of *fat:* milk, cheese, butter. He needs *carbohydrates,* though not in anything like the huge proportion of bland sweet cereal stuffed into the average baby: give him wholewheat bread, potatoes, wholegrain cereal. Health food shops sell special baby-mueslis, or try ordinary Weetabix mashed up in milk. He needs *vitamins A* and *D:* best in cod-liver oil form which doesn't usually make babies throw up though it would us, or else in dropper form. He needs all the *B vitamins* to keep him sweet-tempered and happy, and gets them in liver or wholegrain cereal or yoghurt. He needs *vitamin C:* so give him freshly-pressed orange juice, or mashed ripe peaches, pears, plums, melon, and very lightly cooked vegetables like carrot, broccoli, potatoes, turnips, peas.

He does *not* need extra *sugar:* he eats it anyway in a natural form in fruit or milk. And he particularly doesn't need *salt,* which is positively bad for him, because he might end up absorbing too much sodium. Steer clear, too, of made-up foods stuffed with colouring, preservatives, and so on.

Two particularly good foods for babies are also two of the easiest to feed them. Plain yogurt gives them protein, calcium, Vitamin B; plain cottage cheese gives them protein and calcium.

And yogurt is incredibly simple to make yourself. Here's how. Bring a pint of milk almost to the boil, then let it cool to blood-heat — about quarter of an hour. Pour the milk into a clean bowl, whip in a puddingspoonful of plain firm yogurt, cover the bowl with a clean folded teacloth, and put it in the middle of an oven which has been very slightly warmed by switching on the pilot light, or the warm drawer underneath. In three to five hours, it will have thickened, at which point stick it in the fridge, when it will thicken some more. You can also simply pour the milk-yogurt mix into a wide-necked thermos and leave it for a few hours. And you CAN buy at Boots little sachets of Bulgarian yogurt culture which will make up a quart of incredibly firm yogurt, which will then father about three more nice firm batches before the magic dies out. But the sachets cost about 50p.

Occasionally, and inexplicably, the simple method doesn't work, producing a yucky separated mass instead of a firm cream. Don't worry: it will work the next time.

CHILD'S PLAY

"What would you like for Christmas?" a wealthy friend of ours asked her seven-year-old son.

"I don't really know," he replied politely. "I've got everything I want, thank you".

Unlike grownups, children are seldom interested in possessions for their own sake. They can ignore a whole nurseryful of expensive toys for days on end, concentrating all their love and interest in one grubby old set of building blocks.

And the priciest toys are often the most resounding flops: the elaborately-dressed dolls, the beautifully painted farmyard sets, the huge teddy bear, the complicated peg and board games, the lavish sets of coloured plasticine. The dolls will be undressed and their garments scattered round the nursery; the farmyard sets ignored, the teddy bear left playing second-fiddle to some moth-eaten old duck with its eye hanging out, the plasticine scrunched up into multi-coloured sausages before being ground crumb by crumb into the sitting-room carpet.

No mother, happily, need ever feel guilty at being unable to provide her children with quantities of toys. Far from having a sad deprived childhood, they'll be the lucky children, growing up trained to use their wits, their ingenuity and their imagination.

Under-fives, particularly, are terrible toy-wasters, often casting them aside after one indifferent glance. And there are lots of more effective ways to keep them amused, absorbed and happy, which will hardly cost you a bean, or at worst, won't run you into huge expense.

Small children love water:

They love messing about with it, splashing it around, pouring it out of one container into another. No need to buy them submarines, ducks and Yogi bears for bath-time: just see there's a good supply of old shampoo bottles, yogurt pots and cottage cheese cartons on the bathroom shelf.

Unlike Mummy, children will get fearfully tetchy if you stop them having a go at the washing-up. They aren't, unluckily, much good at it, but that needn't worry either of you as long as you remember to

a) make sure they're securely balanced on chair or whatever in front of the sink, and can't tumble off to crack their heads against the fridge;

b) make sure they can't turn the hot tap on if the water comes out red-hot: give the tap a couple of firm twists to make it proof against child-opening;

c) make sure they can't get at the washing-up liquid and squander the lot in one fell swoop;

d) make sure there isn't any real glass or particularly fragile china around for them to smash.

Give them plenty of supermarket junk — yogurt pots, cottage cheese cartons, and those funny little quilted plates that supermarket meat sits on — and let them get on with it. They'll get soaking wet, of course, but you

can always dry off their clothes. And so will the floor — unless you remembered to put down a newspaper before they started.

Small children love painting:

Partly because they're naturally creative, and partly because it is such a heavenly mess. Alas, that's precisely why most mothers discourage it for most of the time, which seems a great pity. That, and the expense: children don't know how to be economical with their artists' materials. Both mess and expense can, however, be considerably reduced.

Never buy paints in those pricey little children's sets complete with midget-brushes and collapsible-palettes: they'll be used up and hopelessly messed up in the first two goes, and if anyone gives them to your children, pack them firmly away until the children are old enough to use them tidily. Instead, go to your nearest art shop — look it up under Artists' Materials in Yellow Pages — and buy two or three huge tins of non-toxic powder paint. Winsor & Newton do handsome-sized tins for a lot less than a fiver; and for under three pounds you can buy enormous tins which should see your child through to his twenty-first, just about. If you buy a good clear red, a warm yellowy yellow, and a clear blue, you can mix up purple, orange and green yourself — or better still, the children can. And if you throw in white too, a whole range of pastels — for painting on brown envelopes — become a possibility.

Hide the original paint-tins

somewhere where the children can never, ever get at them; decant small quantities into cottage cheese cartons (what would we all do without cottage cheese and yogurt...) of which you have carefully saved the lids; and let the children mix up their own paint on a plate — it's an essential part of the fun.

Paper? It needn't cost you a penny. One of the few advantages of our consumer-bureaucratic society is that for much of the time it simply rains paper. Anyone who works in an office has only to raid the wastepaper basket regularly to come up with fistfuls of wasteful handouts, huge government circulars, tax forms, enormous manila envelopes and so forth. If you don't work in an office, and your husband is inhibited about collecting himself, brazenly ring his secretary and enlist her help. And if anyone in your house sends shirts to the laundry, you'll notice that they very kindly tuck a large stiff sheet of perfect painting paper inside before returning them. Makers of nylon tights do the same thing on a smaller scale. Keep all this lovely un-wastepaper in a special drawer of its own which the children automatically go to: it may discourage them from raiding your writing-desk.

As for the mess, there's not really very much you can do about that, beyond remembering to organise painting sessions before, rather than after, bath-time. You'll find it well worthwhile, however, investing in Mothercare's splendid plastic Playoveralls made for just this purpose: round-necked, ample, with long sleeves elasticised at the wrists, they cost well under a pound, and only need a wipe-down.

Cardboard Boxes:

The five-year-old daughter of one impoverished lady we know, longed and longed for a doll's house. Since bought doll's houses come up pricey, they set about running up their own one rainy afternoon, armed with a big cardboard box. They cut out doors and windows, painted it all bright colours inside and out, stuck on a felt roof. Later, they made furniture out of matchboxes and snippets of cardboard and those paper-covered wire-clips that come in packs of plastic bin-liners; they snipped up bits of fabric for carpets and curtains; cut out mini-pictures from magazines to stick on the walls; and turned oddments of gift-wrap into grand wallpaper. They had a high old time for hours and weeks of rainy days: could any bought dolls' house have given as much continued fun and pleasure?

There are plenty of other uses for those lovable cardboard boxes, which supermarkets kindly donate to their customers, though they charge you for plastic bags. Apart from splendid building material, for instance, they're also excellent storage space.

Keep a big one labelled *CLOTHES FOR DRESSING-UP* if it's little girls you're mainly entertaining. Fill it with the odd long dress, some ridiculously tarty shoes — the tartier the better; a few glittery strings of beads and brooches; any old blouses, scarves, hats.

If you want to know how to keep small children amused for hours on end, with a minimum of commercial toys, take a look at the best-run council Play-group in your neighbourhood. Since it's certainly run on a shoestring, you'll find that the play-material is about ninety percent stuff that you've probably been chucking mindlessly into the dustbin up to now: supermarket meat and vegetable trays, eggboxes, cotton reels, the cardboard rolls that loo-paper is wound on, old tissue boxes, plastic wash-up bottles, boxes and containers of all sizes, shapes, materials. With glue, with paint, and with scissors; with a big working-surface at the children's disposal, and with lots of helpful and encouraging noises

from you, a supply of this kind of super-junk will be worth a hundred pricey plastic animals on a dull afternoon. Keep it all together in another big cardboard box labelled *RAINY DAY*.

Scissors and paste, incidentally, are so basic to good child's play that it's unbelievable how cheap they still are. You can buy safe blunt-ended scissors at Woolworths for about ten pence and huge pots of sweet-smelling Gripfix are also inexpensive if you can't be bothered to make flour and water paste yourself.

Armed with scissors and paste, children can make their own scrapbooks. Keep colour supplements, old Christmas cards, mail-order and store-catalogues, flower catalogues and magazines. One family we know have been keeping huge family scrapbooks for years, since the children were toddlers: into the scrapbooks go photos, tickets, postcards, programmes of plays, letters they wrote each other, drawings, odd small paintings, jokes, special home-made birthday cards.

No child, surely, can have too many books, and children who specially love reading will probably love making their own books. They find the pictures, you all make up the story, and you write it in for them as it goes along. An animal story is a good bet: English newspaper-editors know that the way to their readers' hearts goes straight through the new baby bear at the Zoo: so you'll never be short of picture material.

Sand-pit
A friend of ours reckons that

the three pounds odd she shelled out a few years back on sand was the best investment she ever made: for over four years it kept her small daughter — and lots of her friends — busy and happy out of doors on almost every fine day going. She simply walked into the local builder's yard, bought one yard of sand (that's how they sell it, and it is, she says, exactly the right quantity) paid them three pounds, and they flung it down on the pavement in front of her back door the very next day.

Having picked the right spot for a sand-pit, she hollowed out a big square, lined it with heavy plastic bags so that the sand wouldn't get mixed up with earth when children dug about in it, and put a piece of board neatly down each side. Most of the sand delivered went into a big heap at the back of the garden, from which the sand-pit was refilled from time to time. But even though the sand gets scattered all over the garden, she says, it's not what you might call pollution: the sand simply disappears without trace into the soil.

One word of warning, though: KEEP THE SAND-PIT COVERED WHEN NOT IN USE, lest prowling cats mistake it for a handy bit of litter.

And while we're on the subject of gardens, mothers of darling baby boys should bear in mind that the one thing small boys always, always want to do is kick a ball about. They never want to do it in the lovely park just across the road, either: just right there in the middle of your prize crocuses. "Basically," said the mother of a ten-year-old lad rather crisply, "you have to choose between gardens and children." She hadn't, actually, but we did notice that her flowers tended to be elevated out of harm's way, in big tubs, and that the border plants were tough shrubs: anything fragile or exposed is sheer waste of money until the ball-kicking stage is safely past.

PRESENTS

However impoverished its parents, almost every child gets given presents from time to time: aunts and uncles, grandparents, friends of parents, godparents and so on. Make it clear to them all, as tactfully and persuasively as you can, that books apart, there is one toy that stands alone, and which your children can never have too much of. We refer, of course, to the unique, the incomparable Lego. And since lots of people planning to buy presents for your child simply won't have an earthly what to get him until you tell them, you should soon have a large supply of it at no cost to yourself.

What did parents do before Lego? We simply can't imagine, and neither can most of the parents we know. "The gentle clunk of Lego starts up in early childhood — almost as soon as they're old enough not to keep putting the stuff in their mouths," said one mother of three boys happily. "And it goes on for ever, really. We have a huge drawerful of Lego. Grownups take whole days off work to build battleships with it, and architects plan new towns with it. Its marvellous stuff." No wonder its sales world-wide nearly get to the £100 million mark.

Unlike models — the other great passion of boyhood — great Lego creations can often be recycled: once everyone has admired the battleship to its creator's fill, he will occasionally allow it to be dismantled so that he can start again.

When it comes to your turn for giving presents, to other children of course, Lego is just as good a standby. Another present which never fails to please absolutely anyone — age, interest and occupation regardless — are those rainbow sets of coloured felt-pens which W. H. Smith do ridiculously cheap — much cheaper than anyone else — in several different sizes.

(Note:)

Since last-minute present-buying is usually ruinous present-buying, it's Nouveau Poor sense to keep a large Present Box tucked away somewhere none of the family can get at it easily except you. Keep it stocked with wrapping-paper, Sellotape and coloured ribbon.

Keep a few basic presents for grownups in it, too, for emergencies. We know nobody who doesn't appreciate good soap — Sainsbury's own brand gets so boring eventually — so buy a beautiful box of Roger & Gallet Oeuillet Mignardise, worth the money for the box alone, almost; buy a virile Soap-on-a-Rope for a man; and stock them out of sight and mind in the Present Box. The two other presents that can never miss are booze and money — who can't you give one or the other to, when you come to think of it? — but these are unlikely to lie around in the house unused for long.

ENTERTAINING CHILDREN

When you give a party for your children any time after they're about three-years-old, remember one thing: within their small set, there are already rigid conventions about party-giving. Flout these, and you risk branding your child as a freak and an outsider however amusing the party, because there's no conservative like a baby. In whole huge areas of Great Britain, for instance, we doubt if it's possible to give a really successful small child's party if you don't lay on ample supplies of Smarties at some point in the proceedings. What is it about Smarties? Wouldn't we all like to know?

So before you knock yourself out laying on a splendid entertainment for your child's gang, do a little research to find out what they're actually likely to expect: no use planning a Gourmet Banquet plus conjuror if what they're all currently dotty about is Kentucky Fried Chicken Take-Away Boxes and Blind Man's Buff.

Prevailing conventions apart, here are some guidelines about how to cut out waste on the catering side.

Small children like little bits of food they don't have to fuss about, rather than regimented servings of this and that.

So they like crisps — Marks & Spencer do lots of lovely varieties.

They like tiny little bite-sized

home-made sausage-rolls made with sausage meat padded with plenty of onion and herbs.

They love little cubes of Dutch or Cheddar cheese speared with a bit of pineapple on cocktail sticks but not too sharp, unless you want a massacre on your hands.

And they love small fancy cakes: bake a huge square of plain sponge, cut it into smaller squares, decorate them with different-coloured icings decorated with a Smartie or a Liquorice Allsort.

Don't bother with complicated fancy puddings: fruit jelly to which you add bits of real fruit — orange or banana plus a scoop of ice-cream — are likely to be much more popular.

If you really want to make a big impression, serve ice-cream sodas instead of that horrible bottled fruit stuff: soda water to which you add a spoonful of ice-cream and a drop of Ribena, plus a straw and a long spoon to eat up the ice-cream.

And for the cake, which is the *piece de resistance* at every childish birthday-party: make it decorative but bear in mind that by the time it makes its sensational entry, most of the tiny guests will already have eaten themselves to a standstill. How about a big plain sponge cake with chocolate icing and a snow-white icing Snoopy on top?

THE MIX-MATCHED CHILD

Childless women must wonder why the children of their chic-est friends quite often look such a startling mess.

The answer is perfectly simple: children grow.

They grow relentlessly, stealthily, and in unpredictable spurts.

They grow out of that nice little coat, those good wool trousers, and those wildly expensive shoes. They grow out of clothes so fast that it's possible to come across garments in their cupboard that they've simply never had time to wear. And just as you finally finish putting together some kind of spring wardrobe for them — the star of the show suddenly has to be retired, small.

All of which makes achieving the well-dressed child a hard and costly slog.

Oddly and consolingly enough, it's very slightly easier to do it on a shoestring than with lots of money: you don't get deflected from our masterplan quite so easily.

Here it is:

Rule Number One: Pick out a colour-scheme for your child:

As soon as he or she is into what one might call clothes — as opposed to all-in-one stretch-suits — pick out a colour scheme. Then stick to it, no matter what, for all major buys like coats, jackets, trousers or skirts and shoes. After the first seven years or so, you may very well both be allergic to the specific colours and it will be time for a change: but in the meantime, your child will have looked consistently fairly well put together for most of the time.

An excellent colour-scheme for little girls or boys alike is based on navy, plus red, bright green and yellow, all of which colours also go beautifully with blue denim. (Colours that don't go beautifully with blue denim are right out, anyway.)

Children with their clear skins and bright eyes look particularly good in sizzling combinations of primary colours, as the clever French noted long since: the children's wear department in any big French store is always a cheerful blaze of bright red, yellow, green and navy. And all the bits of this particular scheme work equally well in combination, once you've got it going. The navy dungarees can be worn with red sweater, yellow socks, navy shoes; or green sweater, yellow socks and red shoes; or yellow socks and sweater with navy shoes (which looks amazingly coordinated). So no garment ever languishes wastefully in the children's cupboard because there isn't anything for it to be worn with right now.

Apart from the money this saves you in un-wasted clothes, the time it also rescues for you is beyond belief: no more hours spent dithering at shop counters trying to conjure up a mental review of little Emily's current wardrobe, before you buy her another pair of tights, no more hours spent trying to assemble something decent for morning school.

Navy plus primary colours isn't, of course, the only possible colour-scheme, though we think it takes a lot of beating. According to your personal taste and the looks of your child, you might settle for red, brown, and cream; or red, white, grey and black; or brown, white and yellow; or whatever. And there's nothing to stop you swopping colour-schemes at a well-picked moment when you're all sick to death of the, one you started with. (Switch just before you buy the good new winter overcoat, that's all).

But once you've settled a colour-scheme, stick to it. You will thus avoid having to send your child off to school one uninspired Monday morning wearing brown trousers, navy shoes, a petrol blue and white sweater, and a blue denim jacket, simply because everything else he hasn't grown out of seems to be dirty...

Rule Number Two: Forget skirts and trousers for children under four

All small children have a marked tendency to come apart at the middle; and if you put them into unbraced skirts or unbelted trousers, you can practically guarantee inches of exposed tummy by lunch-time. Tough on a child if its chilly, and instant death to chic.

Instead, put your child into bib-fronted dungarees or pinafore dresses, which simply can't come apart at the waist. What's more, they'll last twice the distance; you can let down the shoulder straps of dungarees as the child grows, notch by notch. And once a skirt is too small, it's very evidently too small; whereas a pinafore dress looks sweet turned into a mini-pinny — especially when you put co-ordinated sweater and tights with it.

Rule Number Three: Never under-estimate your child's rate of growth:

Children grow at an alarming rate, anyway: and they always seem to put on an extra spurt when you're miles away buying clothes for them sight unseen. The coat you thought was enormous, the dress that looked two sizes too big, the dear little jacket that's probably about right all turn out to be — sadly and maddeningly — too small. And there's nothing you can do about it — except vow to buy two sizes too big next time. A child can grow into a mistake on the right side: there's nothing much you can do about clothes that are too small.

Rule Number Four: Pick clothes that grow with a child

One lucky child we know was presented with a soft grey rabbit coat by her godmother when she was five: she was still wearing it with trousers at the age of ten; when she was fourteen, it looked great as a short jacket; and at the age of seventeen she's only just discarded it. The secret? A straight unfussy classic cut; nice long sleeves; generous, slightly dropped shoulders. Children grow upwards much more than sideways, so that any coat you buy them should go on functioning as a jacket for years afterwards, to wear with jeans or trousers, or just kicking around at weekends. If, however, you picked a mimsy little waisted shape, or something tightly tailored — or just a violently colourful pattern you all get sick of fast — you'll be lucky if you get as much as eighteen months' wear out of it.

All children's dresses should have enormously deep hems — you can always run a couple of lengths of colourful rick-rack braiding around to disguise the turned-down tide-mark. Shirts and blouses should have room to spare around chest and shoulders — not to mention adequate sleeve-length. Don't, though, buy your child clothes so absurdly big that he'll be the laughing stock of his class; it's no economy to make him miserable. You can always swap them at the end-of-term-uniform sale, which most schools have. And when you're buying sweaters for a child, look for a generous barrelly shape, dropped shoulder-lines that will ease gently upwards to be a good fit on the shoulder as the child grows; and sleeves long enough to be worn rolled back at first, so that they're a handsome fit eventually. If you're feeling energetic enough to knit this kind of sweater yourself, we've had a basic pattern designed specially for you; a long, long shape, dropped shoulders, low wide crew neck which make it right worn over shirt or without and big barrelly sleeves to allow for lots of growth.

The sweater takes from six 50 gram balls of Jaeger Spiral Spun, a splendid hard-wearing pure English wool double knit. It's made up in easy garter stitch. And there are nearly forty colours to choose from, including all the obvious basics like black, navy, denim, blue, camel, red and grey. Five of the colours are random yarns, mix-ups of several shades of one colour, like the denim-blues we chose for the sweater in the photograph. Random yarns don't show up dirt quite as much...

MATERIALS: Of Jaeger Spiral-Spun Double Knitting, 6[7, 7](50 gram) balls.

Pair each Nos $3\frac{1}{4}$ mm and $4\frac{1}{2}$ mm needles.

Needle sizes quoted are Metric. Equivalent UK sizes are No 10 for $3\frac{1}{4}$ mm and No 7 for $4\frac{1}{2}$ mm.

It is essential to work to the stated tension and Jaeger Handknitting Limited cannot accept responsibility for the finished product if any yarn other than the recommended Jaeger yarn is used.

MEASUREMENTS: To fit chest, 24[26, 28] ins (61[66, 71] cm). Length from top of shoulders, $17\frac{1}{2}[19\frac{1}{2}, 21\frac{1}{2}]$ in (44[49, 54] cm). Sleeve seam, $12\frac{1}{2}[14, 15\frac{1}{2}]$ in (32[36, 39] cm).

SIZES: The figures in square brackets [] refer to the medium and large sizes.

TENSION: 9 sts and 21 rows to 2 in measured over garter stitch on No $4\frac{1}{2}$ mm needles.

ABBREVIATIONS: K = knit; P = purl; st = stitch; tog = together; inc = increase by working into front and back of stitch; dec = decrease by working 2 stitches together; beg = beginning; alt = alternate; in = inches; cm = centimetres; mm = millimetres; M1 = make 1 stitch by picking up horizontal loop lying before next stitch and working into back of it.

BACK

With No $3\frac{1}{4}$ mm needles, cast on 72[76, 80] sts and work in K1, P1 rib for 1 in.

Next row — Rib 3[5, 7], (work 2 tog, rib 5) 9 times, work 2 tog, rib 4[6, 8], (62[66, 70] sts).

Change to No 4½ mm needles and work straight in garter stitch (every row K) until Back measures 11½[13, 14½] in.

Place a marker at each end of last row.

Continue straight until Back measures 16½[18½, 20½] in, endinwith right side facing for next row.

Shape shoulders by casting off 2 sts at beg of next 12 rows, 3[4, 4] sts at beg of following 2 rows, 4[4, 5] sts at beg of following 2 rows.

Leave remaining 24[26, 28] sts on a length of yarn.

FRONT

Work as for Back until 18[18, 20] rows less have been worked before start of shoulder shaping, thus ending with right side facing for next row.

Divide for neck as follows — *Next row* — K26[27, 28], turn and leave remaining sts on a spare needle. Work 1 row.

Dec 1 st at neck edge *only* on next and every following alt row until 19[20, 21] sts remain.

Work 3[3, 5] rows straight, thus ending with right side facing for next row.

Shape shoulder by casting off 2 sts at beg of next and following 5 alt rows, 3[4, 4] sts at beg of following alt row. Work 1 row.

Cast off remaining 4[4, 5] sts.

Leave centre 10[12, 14] sts on a length of yarn, with right side facing rejoin yarn to remaining sts, K to end.

Complete to correspond with first side, reversing shapings.

SLEEVES

With No 3¼ mm needles, cast on 34[36, 38] sts and work in K1, P1 rib for 1 in.

Change to No 4½ mm needles and work in garter stitch, shaping sides by inc 1 st at each end of next and every following 20th[19th, 19th] row until there are 46[50, 54] sts.

Work straight until sleeve seam measures 12½[14, 15½] in.

Cast off loosely.

MAKE UP AND NECKBAND

Do not press.

Join right shoulder.

With right side facing and No 3¼ mm needles, *knit up* 19[20, 21] sts down left side of neck, work across front sts as follows — K3[4, 4], M1, K4[4, 6], M1, K3[4, 4], *knit up* 19[20, 21] sts up right side of neck, work across 24[26, 28] back sts as follows — K3[4, 5], M1, (K2, M1) 9 times, K3[4, 5], (84[90, 96] sts).

Work 7 rows K1, P1 rib.

Cast off evenly in rib.

Join left shoulder seam, neckband, side seams to markers and sleeve seams.

Insert sleeves.

Press seams very lightly following instructions on the ball band. Which brings us instantly to:

Rule Number Five: There is no substitute for wool:

Because in our view, as far as sheer comfort and warmth go, wool takes a lot of beating. And for the kind of rough, tough all-purpose sweater we've had designed for you, which is going to get endless weekend and spare-time wear over years, wool is unbeatable.

Cheap and cheerful man-made fibre sweaters — so bright and tempting on the shop counter, so alluring in their promise of easy-care — have a way of ending up looking merely cheap, we've found all too often. Unless you treat them with the same respect as pure cashmere, they soon start to look tatty and run-down; and whereas well-worn wool still has a certain distinction to it, run-down acrylic or Orlon or nylon starts to look depressingly slummy. By the same token, however, man-mades are fine for short-term wear; so if you want just one nice cheap sweater to fill a temporary gap, you're probably better off with an acrylic.

Rule Number Six: Chain-stores are for children:

In economic terms, how can chain-stores not have an edge over any other source of children's wear? They're cutting those easy, straightforward shapes by the hundred thousand: if they can't do them twice as cheap as the shop around the corner or Harrods, they're robbing their customers blind. Luckily, they aren't. Even more luckily, styling in at least one chain of stores — Marks & Spencer — is now crisp, colourful and on the whole very good indeed; in C & A, British Home Stores and Littlewoods it's occasionally very good, or at least in patches; and the inimitable Mothercare have now extended their range up to ten-years-old.

Bright fleece-lined coats or practical anoraks and one-piece weather-suits; simple cotton cord dungarees or snappy wool tartan skirts; colourful tights and socks in plain stitches, good primary colours; jolly summer cottons and amusing winter sweaters; practical towelling pyjamas in vivid colours and prints; cosy fleecy dressing-gowns... It's difficult to think of one area of child's wear that isn't covered by chain-stores, one way or another. And if you go abroad on holiday, ear-mark a spot of your foreign currency for a foray into the biggest local chain-store. *Upim* in Italy, for instance, has absurdly jolly colours for tiny tots, and a year ago, they were still selling pure cotton socks, a luxury that seem to have been retired for good elsewhere in Europe. And *Prisunic* in France sell French dash and chic at absurdly child-sized prices: one of our friends always comes back from Paris loaded with their blue denim dungarees, with adjustable metal braces, at around two pounds fifty, and with their pure cotton vests for about a pound in primary red, blue and yellow, or red and white stripes, that double up as T-shirts for summer wear.

Rule Number Seven is a Foot-Note:

You can't economise on shoes — because everyone knows a child's feet can be permanently damaged or distorted by wearing badly-fitting shoes. You can, though, save on actual wear by encouraging your child to run around bare-foot when at home in reasonable warmth, or out of doors in the garden as long as it isn't frosty or soaking wet. It's lovely for the children, it's heaven for their feet — and it saves that pricey shoe-leather from needless wear and tear.

The Flexible Adaptable Switcharound Home

The FLEXIBLE ADAPTABLE SWITCHAROUND HOME

With a few good ideas, you can do up a whole house for the price of a three-piece suite, a fitted kitchen and a cocktail cabinet. And you won't be needing any of those, for a start.

Most important: make the space in your house or flat really work and that means forgetting the traditional assumption that bedrooms are for sleeping, dining rooms for eating and sitting rooms for relaxing or entertaining. "Rooms should be so versatile you can change them about when you feel like it, or even completely alter their function," says Juliet Glyn Smith. "So, keep the incredible fluorescent pinks for the loo or the spare bedroom and have a very simple, undemanding scheme in the areas where you spend most of your time."

Juliet and her husband design hotels, restaurants and houses as well as the delightful Hunkydory range of stationery. She says she is constantly changing her home about as her children get older. "You do need various areas for doing things. An area where the grownups can get away by themselves and have lovely things and where the children won't knock about and break everything, a place where older children can do their homework in peace.

"Even in a semi you could work it so that the kitchen cum dining room is a knockabout place and the front room is kept for the grownups, like an old-fashioned parlour. As the children grow, you can turn their bedrooms into bed-sits. Bedrooms are a dreadful waste of space if they are hardly ever used and the bedroom can be the best possible bolthole, study and relaxing room for parents."

How to plan for an easy switch-around? "Take one colour right through the house," says designer and architect Max Clendinning: "It's cheaper to buy a great deal of one colour than lots of different little pots of paint. So many people start off thinking: 'If we have the bathroom blue and the bedroom pink, will the brown carpet in the sitting room look all right with blue and the pink, and what about the lamps...?' and they have doubled both the cost and the confusion. One colour looks much nicer and it means that all your decorations are completely interchangeable."

Keep everything flexible, with adjustable shelves, room dividers and stacking drawers so you can alter the size of the rooms by pushing back a divider and shuffling things about to get the best possible arrangement at any given time. One of the most practical study bedrooms we've ever seen had a great big bed, piled with cushions, a couple of workman-like table desks in the window and the washbasin, dressing table, clothes cupboards and paraphernalia were all hidden away on one wall behind a series of louvre doors. If you can't afford the louvres, you could always use cheap pinoleum blinds as a cover-up or curtain it the same colour as the walls. The bedroom is now a children's playroom and the louvre doors usefully conceal even more unsightly mess. It is, incidentally, often enlightened self-interest to give the children the biggest room in the house where they can sleep, watch telly and run riot, while you — hopefully neater — can slot peacefully into something smaller.

KITCHENS

Don't be beguiled by the Ideal Kitchens in the telly ads., with lovely Mum flitting happily from work surface to work surface and matching cupboards climbing along and up every bit of available wall space. Clearly, the carefree Mum did not have to foot the bill, because this kind of kitchen costs a bomb and, no matter how folksy you may get with strings of garlic and onions, it remains so determinedly clinical that you can't pretend it's a dining room; not that there's room for anything but a bar counter with uncomfortable stools to fall off over breakfast, once you've ranged all those fitments around the walls.

The nicest kitchens are roomy, with low, open shelves so you can grab at the everyday necessities, one huge cupboard or dresser, concealing the dust collectors, a large kitchen table which is useful for painting and homework as well as eating, and a comfortable chair and bottle of plonk for the cook. You can still find big, deal farmhouse tables for around twenty pounds in the second-hand furniture warehouses and, so long as you aren't after the pretty, Welsh antique variety, dressers and sideboards abound in the second-hand shops, and simple chairs cost only two pounds apiece. If you don't care for a shiny veneer, or want to remove the paint, use Strypit and finish with a professional polish of Briwax (a trick of the trade, available at 34, Blythe Road, W.14 and 107-115, Long Acre, W.C.2. or write to the Manufacturers, Bromel Paint Mills,

Croydon Road, Elmers End, Beckenham, Kent). Strippers, the furniture sort, advertise in *Time Out* and local papers and they will do the job for a few pounds.

The curious fashion of dropping ovens and hobs all around the kitchen, at enormous cost, so that you have to zig-zag about, checking a veg here, stirring a sauce there and basting a joint somewhere else, reached its peak when a Gas Board executive recently told us proudly that they had found an ingenious way of placing all the component bits next to each other: "Ah," we said. "We used to call that a cooker."

It's a bit of a cliché, but nevertheless true, that the most vital piece of kitchen gadgetry is a very sharp knife. After that it's any piece of Moulinex equipment. We've noticed that people who own the most elaborate mixers rarely use them because they are such hell to wash, but Moulinex gadgets are blissfully simple and cheap. They also do a first-class after-sales service, stocking the parts for machines which went out of production years ago. Indesit have the same sort of reputation for economy and simplicity, and those of us who own one of their washing machines or dish washers find that they hardly ever go wrong, a shrewd argument in their favour when it can cost nine pounds twenty five pence plus VAT just to let a repairman through the door. Get your own back by always having an appliance serviced the week before the guarantee runs out.

PLAN BEFORE YOU BUY ANYTHING

Top designer, Max Clendinning, thinks that most homes have too much furniture: "A room looks most magnificent when it's empty except for one flower in a pot, one perfect picture, something beautiful to look at. Don't even buy a chair until you have carefully considered: 'Do I need it? Do I like it? Is it going to add to the room?'"

The best way of planning what you need and fitting in the things you already have, is to draw a scale plan of your rooms and make cut-outs of the furniture. This will avoid the nasty scene as you say: "Why don't we put the sofa over by the fire where it was and try the table back here?" If Granny's old three-piece doesn't fit into your scheme of things, chuck it out. This will work out cheaper than forever re-upholstering it, throwing bits of patchwork over it or buying expensive cushions and covers trying to disguise it.

A clever way to get instant seating is to build a wooden platform along one side of a room or in a bay window, cover it with an old carpet and pile it up with giant cushions.

Dunlopillo, latex foam (which is cheaper) and Pirelli rubber webbing are the greatest aids for amateur upholsterers who aren't prepared to go to evening classes and learn how to do the thing properly. You can buy bags of foam offcuts for around thirty pence to fill cushions, make an effective sack chair by three-quarter filling a large bag with expanded polystyrene granules, stick layers of Dunlopillo or foam together for a bed or a lounging seat. (Put them on wooden bases if low level lounging isn't your style.) Model girl Vicki Hodge, who likes to lounge, has turned a small basement room into a miracle of seductive comfort with exotic carpets, lamps and small tables, piles of tapestry, velvet and carpet cushions and the whole thing topped by a silky tent, draped down to the floor from a central brass ring. It saved her redecorating the walls, too. More prosaically, if you've bought or inherited a sofa or chaise-longue with sagging springs, just whip them out and criss-cross Pirelli webbing tightly across the wooden base, building up the seat with layers of foam. Not madly springy but comfortable enough.

SECOND-HAND FURNITURE

Second-hand furniture is usually more attractive and solidly made than most of the astronomically priced new furniture in the stores. But, where do you find the bargains? Alas, there aren't many left. We canvassed a dozen antique and second-hand dealers who all agreed they couldn't afford to buy at auctions and country sales any more because even quite nasty stuff is bought at huge prices, done up and shipped off abroad. Since all the dealers are now wise to the "Suffolk run", the "Barrow in Furness run" and all the other fruitful out-of-town bargain trips, you are as likely to find cheap second-hand furniture in London or any big town, as in a remote country village.

The trick is to spot the potential in the unlikeliest pieces. Two old wooden filing cabinets, for instance, make a good desk if they are topped by a thick plank. Timber merchants will cut to size to save your fingers and temper. Wrought-iron Victorian lavatory cistern brackets give a luxury look to cheap shelving and even metal industrial shelving looks okay if you paint it the same colour as the walls. Saw the legs off an old dining table, paint it a glossy bright colour, coat the top with stain and heat resisting transparent polyurethane varnish and you've got a great coffee table.

All this sawing and platform building may sound difficult but it's a lot easier than putting together the aptly named knockdown (sometimes less aptly called quick-assembly) furniture which you take home in bits and pieces and assemble yourself. After one assembler ran screaming from his fragments of wardrobe, his wife called in a professional carpenter and joiner who then took two days to get the kit together. Another kit victim is still working on his wardrobe, some eight years after his original agonised assembly, since every time a child runs merrily across the floor the cupboard slides gently apart again.

Those firms advertising in the Colour Supplements — Why Not Enjoy this Delightful Tea Service/Reproduction Coffee Table in the Comfort of Your Own Home etc — really do have bargains. A set of bronze cutlery bought this way was *half* the price of the equivalent cutlery in a shop. But, do check furniture sizes carefully before ordering. A sofa that appears to be capacious enough for the three in the picture can turn out hardly bigger than a smallish armchair.

If you're looking for modern second-hand bargains, a bike, pram, table tennis table, fridge and so on, invest in the *Exchange & Mart* which comes out every Thursday and makes an intriguing read even if they haven't got what you want in their ads. What was J.S.F. of Exeter *doing* with the four Japanese swords he's anxious to swap for a complete set of the *Boys Own Paper?*

PUTTING IT ALL TOGETHER

This sends most people into a trauma of self-doubt. Possibly it's the home writers' constant cry of "Do your own thing! Your home should reflect your personality" which makes us pause and wonder what we might be revealing if we did up our bedrooms in icy pale blue.

"So many people get a sort of Decorating Compulsion and go around stores, clutching a piece of carpet and a piece of curtain trying to find the *exact* matching orange upholstery," says home and design writer Janet Fitch. "They desperately try to make things "Go" when actually, if they stick to neutral colours — a range of browns and beiges, for instance — it doesn't really matter very much."

Janet is married to Design Consultant Rodney Finch and they have just moved into a lovely old house in Wiltshire. "Being a designer, Rodney is always far too busy thinking about his clients' problems to give a lot of time to his own house," says Janet. "'Where is everyone going to hang their coats?' I kept saying and Rodney said he'd think about that later. The result is a pile of coats and anoraks in the hall because the children can't reach the afterthought bentwood hatstand. Moral: think about vital things like spaces for hooks and the positioning of electric light points *before* and not *after* you decorate."

If you don't trust yourself to stay tastefully and economically within a simple colour range, a cunning ruse is to do small rooms in a solid block of colour or pattern — the ceiling, the chests, the cupboards, too. We've found that although putting fabric on the walls costs more than wallpaper it still looks like new ten years later. Forget all that wooden battening bit. You can stick it on the walls with ordinary Polycell water paste, leaving a slight overlap for shrinkage. Habitat have the most original and attractive wallpapers and they are often cheaper than the equivalent Marks and Spencer wallpapers. On the whole, though, wallpaper and fabric are expensive, horrid to hang and, when you try and replace a bit of it you'll almost certainly hear "Buttercup? Oh, we discontinued that pattern *years* ago." Woolworths and Tesco do nice paints in good colours at a reasonable price. Emulsion paint is cheap and a good quality one washes again and again. John Oliver at 33, Pembridge Road, London, W.11. will mix paint to an exact match if you send him a colour swatch. If you have to cover a bad wall, go for one of those bobbly "relief" papers to camouflage the uneven plasterwork and then emulsion it.

BUY THE BEST QUALITY CARPET AND UNDERLAY YOU CAN AFFORD

If you can only afford a tiny area of close-fitting luxury put it in the bathroom for maximum effect. There are several carpet warehouses selling cheap offcuts, but if you are looking for a particular colour or quality and quite a lot of it, stores like John Lewis, Whiteleys and the Civil Service Stores are sometimes cheaper.

Good wood floors can be sanded down and then painted with transparent polyurethane. It's easy enough to hire a sander (look for the Hire Shops in Yellow Pages) but tough doing the sanding with sawdust, old bits of paint and dirt flying up your nose and into your hair. Bare boards can be chilly, too, and we prefer the idea of covering kitchens, play rooms and children's rooms in cheerful tile-patterned lino and putting haircord or rubber-backed carpeting everywhere else. Cork tiles often work out as expensive as carpet and although rush matting and the

sisal sort of carpeting are satisfactory in a kitchen, it's a mistake anywhere you expect to place a bare knee or foot.

Once you've got the basic cheap floor covering, add mats and carpets as you get the money. Auction sales are still useful for second-hand carpets and Simmonds, a second-hand shop in Gower Street, just near Euston, usually have excellent 12' x 9' carpets for less than £50. You have to heave through the stock and clean the carpet when you get home but, as the ad. used to sing, "1001 cleans a big, big carpet for less than half a crown". If you're anxious about moth, wipe the carpet over with a touch of white spirit. "What *do* you imagine people did before aerosols?" a hardware store owner asked us scathingly, when we were searching around for a mothproofing spray.

Glamorous goat-hair rugs get cheaper daily but *don't* be tempted as they shed more hairs than half a dozen white Persian cats. If you're fond of hairy rugs, go for the Greek wool ones which can be washed or put into an automatic dry cleaner.

CURTAINS

Curtains look good and shut out the draughts (and, incidentally, those of us who can't afford double glazing, tape up all but one of the windows in each room with Cling draught-excluder strip around November and unpeel it in April) but blinds take less fabric and don't need lining or interlining. All the John Lewis branches have do-it-yourself roller blind kits and sell the stiffened fabric, too. You could try using ordinary fabric and stiffening it with the aerosol spray that is sold for the purpose, but we did and it didn't work.

Pinoleum blinds cost less than any others but only look happy in ethnic-peasant or ultra-modern-white-Formica decors. Instead of curtains or blinds, brighten up a window with strings of brightly-coloured beads, with shelves of attractively shaped and coloured bottles, or turn the whole window area into a greenhouse of plants, with hanging baskets, a trellis of jasmine and giant pots of indoor plants.

Plants and books are the easiest, nicest form of decoration and both Woolworth and Marks & Spencer stock an exotic selection of indoor plants. Overwatering is more likely to kill than forgetting to water them but, even if a plant withers and droops within a month, it's still cheaper than buying cut flowers. A group of plants, massed together in old china vegetable dishes and pots, is a perfect cover-up for an empty or ugly grate, an interesting focal point on a low, pretty table.

HOW ABOUT LIGHTING?

It's the biggest potential disaster area of all and bad, unsymmetrical pathetic and impractical lighting can ruin a relationship as well as your eyes. Who wants to stay home and read in the evenings if, when they curl comfortably on the sofa, they can't actually *see* and who would care to dine nightly opposite a loved one consistently bathed in a harsh, unflattering light?

"Decide on the function of a room and light it accordingly," says lighting consultant, Janet Turner. "If it's a family room with different activities going on, light up the areas people actually use. There's a very good economic argument for using track — British Home Stores sell millions of feet of it now — because you can move it around, take it with you if you move, put spots in and take them out as you need them.

"Buy a length of track, put it on the ceiling if the room is high, on the wall if it's a low ceiling and start with just one directional spot. Then, see how much more light you need, where you want it, what you want it for and gradually add the necessary spotlights. You may need a subdued spot to cast a pleasant glow around the room, a strong, small-beam directional light over a chair for reading, a framing spot (Concord Lighting International sell them) which adjusts to exactly frame a picture. No matter how many pretty lamps there are in a room, it needs the drama of a spot to accentuate a painting or a loved object, to really bring the room alive.

"Spots are even more useful in a bedroom. If one person wants to read and the other is fretfully trying to get to sleep, you should have a small-beam spot that just shines onto the page and nothing around it. Nearly all mirror lighting is hopeless. When you're shaving or doing your face you don't need light on the mirror but on you; a milky pearl bulb so it doesn't glare into your eyes. The ideal is to re-create the make-up table in the star's dressing room at the Palladium."

Janet says lots of people are put off spotlights because they don't feel it goes with antique furniture: "Not true. I've got tracks all over my old Victorian house and they look marvellous. Of course, you can't dictate to people about lighting; the thing is to put lights where you need them and whatever kind you like. I think those old-fashioned jingley Chinese lanterns are lovely — and very cheap."

So they are. And so are almost all the light fittings at British Home Stores. Their range is enormous, their prices so low it takes your breath away and the designs up-to-date with super Tiffany copies selling for less than a fiver.

It would, of course, be even nicer to own the genuine article. We know a girl who spotted a near-Tiffany in a shop window eight years ago for twenty-five pounds and decided she couldn't afford it. The other day she wept to see the exact twin in another shop at £300 pounds. "It isn't the money you spend you regret, it's the money you don't spend," we're always saying, recklessly signing another cheque.

But good carpets *do* last longer. Antiques *are* an investment. And, if you don't get that beautiful picture when you see it, it *will* be gone.

Don't buy it – Grow it

DON'T BUY IT
- GROW IT

Whether you've got a garden, terrace, balcony or just a grotty dustbin area christened "patio" by your estate agent, now is the time to lay your hands on some earth and get growing. It's soothing, healthy and a marvellous money-saver.

Suppose you've got six friends coming to dinner: by the time you've bought some artichokes, fennel, chicory, French beans, a few herbs, the *mange-touts* to go with your lamb and the garlic to stick into it, plus a couple of bunches of flowers, there won't be much change from a fiver. For that money you could buy enough seeds to grow these sort of luxury greengrocery items in your garden and you could feed your family and friends on them for a whole year.

It's madness to go out and buy flowers when you can grow them, cheap stews taste expensive with the addition of home-grown herbs, and fruit from your own tree has far more vitamins than the flavourless Granny Smith that spent God knows how long getting here from New Zealand.

PLANNING

Make the most of every inch of earth you've got, and that means planning. If you haven't got much room, paving makes more sense than grass. You can leave spaces between large irregular stones and put plants in them, and stand tubs, boxes, and all sorts of containers about the place so that you get more growing area. If you've taken over an old garden, there are probably trees around, but remember that you can't make your garden productive unless you've got plenty of light, air and with any luck, sun, so just keep any really beautiful specimens, and then clear your space for action.

You can't grow anything without good earth, so feed it like mad. Apart from making friends with anyone who has a cow, horse or pig who can supply you with the real stuff, it's a good idea to make your own compost. Good husbandry, this; you just pile up any old vegetable rubbish — potato peelings, tea-leaves, dead flowers, cabbage stalks — sprinkle it with a magic substance quaintly named Garotta, and soon you'll have lovely brown crumbly goodness to work into your soil. If you haven't the room for this performance, sprinkle on a bit of bonemeal in the autumn, National Growmore in the spring, heave in a bale of peat (all available from your local Woolworth's or ironmonger) and your soil will be in what is known cheerily as "good heart".

When you consider what to plant, try and choose things which combine loveliness with usefulness. If you fancy planting a tree or two in a bare new plot, make it a mini-orchard and plant apple, plum or pear, then you've got blossom in the spring, harvest in the autumn, and as they mature, privacy from the neighbours. Careful when you choose your fruit trees; they too want a satisfying sex-life and unless their cross-pollination is looked into, you won't get much fruit. However, one obliging apple called James Grieve has strange habits and will produce young all by itself.

SHRUBS
It's worth investing in some background shrubs. Study some catalogues, visit your local garden centre. Shrubs may seem expensive, but once they're in — that's it. They grow bigger every year, give your garden or terrace shape and substance, and you need never be without something to pick and bring into the house all through the year. Just a few suggestions: have some evergreens — by which we don't mean gloomy, expensive and dust-gathering rhododendrons — so that you don't look out of the window at bare earth and twigs half the year; get a Viburnum Tinus, which grows like crazy even in the shade, has attractive green leaves and the bonus of pinky-white heads of flowers which actually bloom in the winter. Choisya Ternata, is another evergreen which grows very fast in a cosy, sheltered position and in May is covered in scented white flowers. Senecio Greyii keeps its silvery felted leaves all the year, and is nice for picking. Have a Forsythia; it grows quickly, you can bring a few sprigs inside in deepest winter and the yellow flowers will open in the warmth of the room, then in March the bush will be a heart-warming splash of gold. *Any* leaves put in a wine-glass make a few solitary daffodils look like a sophisticated Japanese flower arrangement.

ROSES
Don't use precious space for rose bushes, much as we love them. Better to get climbing ones to cover your fences and walls, easy growers like Mermaid, a lovely single yellow rose with almost evergreen leaves; Schoolgirl, with its sensational apricot colour and ravishing scent; and

New Dawn, palest shell-pink. They're all prolific and flower at different times of the summer, so you'll always have a single rose to put in a glass on your table. No need to send off to some grand rose specialist; we have very good reports of twenty-two pence specimens bought at Woolworths. Mix them up with other climbing plants like clematis (Jackmanii is a lovely deep purple, and dead easy) and the best bargain plant of all, the honeysuckle called Lonicera Halliana. It's evergreen, spreads all over the place, flowers from June through to November, and smells simply divine.

LAYING OUT THE GARDEN

Forget everything you've heard about dividing a garden into flower-beds, vegetable plots and herb gardens. Make yours the ultimate in cottage gardens, with all sorts of plants crammed together; they don't mind living in crowded conditions as long as you feed them well. Think in terms of light and shadow. If there's a very shaded bit, make it grotto-like; not with mournful laurels which cost a fortune, but with ferns (always carry a trowel about your person when going for country walks), and common old ivy pinned down with hairpins as it grows to cover the ground with a shiny green carpet. Put in bluebells for the spring, and sprinkle foxglove seeds which will come up every summer happily ever after. Bay and mint don't mind a bit of shade, nor do alpine strawberries — lovely little plants with white flowers, and sweet berries if you

can move faster than the local bird population.

Make the most of warm, sunny corners. This is where your tomato plants go. Try them in a Gro-bag — you can get about four plants into the rich, black peaty mixture, and with a lot of watering and loving care you should get pounds of tomatoes. Herbs need sunshine, too. Make a background of rosemary, sage, lavender and thyme, and in between them you can plant the seeds of the bright annual flowers which need the sun: marigolds, nasturtiums, love-in-a-mist, candytuft, — old-fashioned flowers which are easy to grow and lovely for picking. What's more they seed themselves from year to year and pop up all over the garden. You'll probably want a few permanent things like lupins and marguerites, but they're not sacred. Have a clump

of beetroots among them with their gorgeous foliage, and sprinkle some spinach seed in empty spaces — a gratifying veg to cultivate, this, as the more you pick its bright green leaves, the more it grows. Carrots have got pretty, feathery green tops, and make a nice edging to a bed. Parsley, too which incidentally we always found difficult to get started until a learned horticultural friend told us that there are certain plants which take to each other and make good bed-fellows, parsley and roses being one such happy marriage. Sure enough, ever since we put the parsley at the foot of the climbing Mermaid, it's gone like a bomb.

Unless you've got lots of space, there's no point in yearning for vast cabbages and rows of onions. But salads are easy to fit in. Sprinkle just a *few* lettuce seeds, a *few* radish and spring onion seeds in spots where they get some sun. Keep them watered and thinned out, then about three weeks later, sprinkle a few more somewhere else. That way you won't be landed with thirty-eight lettuces ready to eat on one day in June, and none for the rest of the summer. Runner beans are smashing things to grow, with their pretty scarlet flowers first, then masses of beans which seem to grow as fast as you pick them. Grow them wigwam fashion: push three bamboo poles into the earth at the back of a border and secure them at the top, plant your beans at the foot of the poles, give them plenty of water and there'll be no holding them. Dwarf French beans are very rewarding in not much space, and courgettes are a cinch if you feed and water them well — but do keep a wary eye on them. One thoroughly irresponsible gardener we know was foolhardy enough to go on holiday just when the dear little things were

nearing their time. She paled beneath her tan when she got home to find a positive crêche of infant-sized vegetable marrows lying smugly looking up at her. There are limits to friendship, she discovered, as she begged people to lug the monsters away.

If you dream of self-sufficiency, and have visions of yourself hoeing between orderly rows of brassicas and roots, try getting yourself an allotment. They're very difficult to come by, but you could be one of the fortunate few. Track down your Allotment Association by ringing the Local Council or the Town Hall. For something like seventy-five pence a year you'll have a plot nearly the size of a tennis-court to sow and reap, so it's worth having a go. Just think, you'll be able to go berserk with armies of sweet corn, serried ranks of kohl rabi and salsify, and bushels of precious potatoes.

But don't be down-hearted if you haven't even got a backyard. A sunny window-box can be stuffed with salads. Tomatoes do very well in big clay flowerpots, and one of the prettiest balconies we know has not only masses of flowers, but clusters of flower pots planted with all sorts of herbs — tarragon, basil, chives, lemon-balm.

YOU DON'T HAVE TO SPEND A LOT OF MONEY ON GARDENING

It's supposed to *save* you money, remember?

Never buy boxes of plants and go in for all that senseless "bedding-out" routine; just forget geraniums, salvias, petunias and lobelia — you can spend about thirty pounds on boxes of miserable little green sprouts which may or may not do well, and next year you'll have to start all over again.

Grow everything you can from seed. Woolworth seeds are great value, in fact many country gardeners swear by them. Carter's seeds are good and come in beautifully designed packets. Not only are they pretty, but they give you complete growing instructions — a little gardening lesson with each pack, so even the rawest recruit can't go wrong.

Read good gardening books and learn how to propagate plants for yourself — once you've got the knack of taking cuttings, you don't have to buy any more shrubs.

Cultivate gardening friends. All gardeners respond most favourably to flattery, and all you need to do is gasp, "that is the most stunning veronica I ever saw — how *do* you do it!" and in the twinkling of a secateur you will find yourself in possession of a nice healthy little cutting. They're generous folk, most of them, and will be only too pleased to give you a forkful of campanula which is rampaging around and strangling their roses.

TOOLS

You're going to need tools for all this tilling of the soil, but that doesn't mean you have to rush out and buy stainless steel at exorbitant prices. Consider how hard you're going to work them. If you're one of the lucky ones with an allotment, you'll need quite solid spade, fork, rake and hoe, but don't get carried away — the medium price range made by Spears and Jackson are good value and if you look after them by cleaning them after the day's labour, and occasionally wiping them with an oily rag, they'll last for years. If it's window-box pottering you're going for, then a cheap range of tools is good enough. Just don't expect too much from them; even wrestling with a stubborn pot of ivy can cause a cheap trowel to bend gently in the middle.

Come the winter don't give up the good work. Grow mustard and cress on a damp flannel, bean sprouts on blotting-paper like you did at school (they make a lovely winter salad with vinaigrette dressing), bring some herbs indoors in pots, and dry bay leaves and thyme for winter soups. And before you know where you are, the crocuses will be popping up outside and it'll be time to get back to your digging.

Spend Traps

SPEND TRAPS –
Fifty Ways To Lose A Fiver (Or More)

1. Go shopping with a dear friend.
2. Buy lots of coloured wool and start a tapestry cushion.
3. Pay the grocery bill by cheque.
4. Order steak from the butcher when you can't think of anything else for dinner.
5. Commute.
6. Buy a child more than one pair of shoes at a time.
7. Do all your household shopping after work at the late-night delicatessen.
8. Go out and celebrate a £4 pools win.
9. Lay in 20 lbs. of sugar next time you hear a rumour it's going to be scarce.
10. Bleach your hair.
11. Order four cases of whisky because you've heard it's going up 2p. a bottle in the Budget.
12. Have a facial.
13. Believe the shoe-shop assistant who says: "Don't worry,
they'll stretch."
14. Join a Health Club.
15. Grab the funny-coloured Missoni sweater that doesn't *quite* fit because it's been reduced by £5.
16. Telephone all your friends before lunch.
17. Up-date a dreary old evening dress with a new pair of Jourdan velvet shoes.
18. Take taxis to save time.
19. Snap up $1\frac{1}{4}$ metres of costly fabric because it's Bound to Come In.
20. Overtip waiters so they'll remember you next time.
21. Fill every available vase with fresh flowers to impress guests who always bring them.
22. Give pots of home-made marmalade to all your friends.
23. Wait at least two weeks before sending your hostess a "thank you" note, so you have to include a dozen red roses.
24. Run the Tombola for

the school fete.

25. Get a bank loan to pay for an overdraft.
26. Forget a friend's birthday so you can rush out and buy him a last-minute bottle of champagne.
27. Buy cheap saucepans.
28. Give the children exciting gifts because you've been out three nights running.
29. Use paper napkins rather than linen ones.
30. Run the dishwasher when it's only half full.
31. Give every small present a luxury touch with glossy, patterned gift wrappings.
32. Send your sweaters to the dry cleaners.
33. Lose the refunds on railways tickets by tucking them into a very safe place you can't remember.
34. Take old scuffed shoes to be heeled *and* soled.
35. Forget to return library books.
36. Play Monopoly with pesetas, drachma and other foreign currencies as they aren't real money.
37. Open an account.
38. Buy a house in Spain and save on hotel bills.
39. Lose your share certificates.
40. Rush out and buy a complete set of co-ordinated beachwear just before going on holiday.
41. Hire an accountant.
42. Avoid claiming government grants because it's a bore getting the relevant forms together.
43. Buy a dog.
44. Invest in a country cottage so you don't need to spend on foreign holidays.
46. Get a leotard to encourage you to do early morning exercises.
47. Give up smoking, then decide to have just the occasional tiny cigar.
48. Have your after-dinner mints hand-made at Fortnums because You Get What You Pay For.
49. Save up for a mink because It's an Investment.
50. Serve champagne because It's Cheaper in the Long Run.

Look it up Here

LOOK IT UP HERE

1. THE CLOTHES FILE

Dressmaker by Ann Ladbury, BBC Publications, £2.40. You can now buy the book of the T.V. programme. Even the most ham-fisted will be able to make simple, chic clothes with these detailed, step-by-step instructions. Paper patterns are inserted in a pocket at the back of the book, and you have the basics of a super wardrobe — T-shirt, trousers, skirt, and a lovely shirtwaister, plus suggestions on variations on the themes.

Penguin Book of Sewing by Julian Robinson, £1.50, illustrated by Renée Robinson. This husband and wife team are lecturers on fashion and design, which gives their book a lot of style. They aim to show that sewing can be fun.

Dressmaking by Isabel Horner, in the Teach Yourself Series by Hodder and Stoughton, 40p. Illustrated book, including how to use a machine, choose fabrics, use a paper pattern.

EVENING INSTITUTE CLASSES. Look up your local classes; they include budget dressmaking, creative dressmaking, "dolly bird" dressmaking, pattern cutting, and dress design.

STREET MARKETS. Keep an eye on clothes stalls in your local market, as they quite often have seconds and left over stock from well-known manufacturers like Harold Ingram, Jump, Stirling Cooper. Especially good in this line for Londoners is the market at Petticoat Lane, E.1. — it's near Liverpool Street Station, open Sundays, 9 am — 2 pm.

JANNABAGS 18, Samantha Close, Walthamstow, London, E.17. Mail-order only, so send for a list of their super handbags at low prices. Canvas, denim and others — a roomy attractive shoulder-bag with zips and pockets in faded blue denim is £5.78.

WESTAWAY AND WES-TAWAY, 65 Great Russell Street, London, W.C.1. Unique shop, crammed with beautiful tartans, shetlands, cashmere sweaters, Fair Isle mittens and caps, gossamer wool shawls, tweeds — all British luxury goods, but cheaper than you can buy anywhere else. The place is jam-packed with foreign tourists, English hardly spoken except by the impeccable Mr. Westaway himself. They sell enormous quantities, mainly abroad, and their prices are geared to the overseas market. No mail-order in this country, alas, but they will send you a catalogue and it's well worth a visit when you're in London — bang opposite the British Museum too.

LAURENCE CORNER, 62/64 Hampstead Road, London, N.W.1., Tel: 01-387 6134. This famous mecca for London trendies and their kids, now do mail-order. Now their legendary jeans, army greatcoats, tough sweaters — all at low prices and stylish because of their basic quality — can be sent to you by post. They will send you a catalogue if you write to the above address, and a broadsheet covering items in their Him and Her Boutique, 126, Drummond Street, N.W.1.

PIXIE, 329 Fulham Road, London, S.W.10. Tel: 01-352-4433. You can go to the shop, but their main business is mail-order. Their very pretty and unusual clothes are exclusive to them. Utterly feminine styles in muslin, lawn, calico — and very cheap. They send out a catalogue if you write or 'phone.

OASIS TRADING, 24, Little Clarendon Street, Oxford.

Mail-order but with a retail shop at the above address in Oxford, this firm specialises in marvellous ethnic clothes at reasonable prices. They import hand-made things like Peruvian knitwear (£1 for a pair of natural wool gloves) leather bags, belts and sandals from Morocco; wrap-over skirts in hand-printed fine cotton from India; wooden and glass bangles and beads. Write to them for details of lots more lovely, inexpensive and individual clothes.

ANELLO AND DAVIDE, 35, Drury Lane, W.C.2; 96 Charing Cross Road, W.C.2. Old-established firm who make shoes for theatre and ballet. You can buy what they call "Character" shoes in leather, pretty style with medium heel and bar over the instep, for as little as £6.75.

Next door at 30 Drury Lane, is the **FACTORY SHOP** — where they are selling all sorts of boots and shoes at very cut prices — something which was £16 is now under £10. Personal shoppers only.

THE LAST PICTURE FROCK, Pembridge Road, London, W.11. Ken Russell's wife, Shirley, is selling here not only ravishing antique clothes, but also has dresses used in films and T.V. plays — a marvellous way to bargain glamour.

JUST A SECOND, 10 Queensway, London, W.2. All new stock, but end of line or rejects. Very good for separates, and cheap.

THE FROCK EXCHANGE, 450 Fulham Road, London, S.W.6. Second-hand, but only very up-to-date clothes and well-known makes. Even when reduced Thea Porter and Jean Muir clothes are not cheap, but certainly bargain price here. And they do have inexpensive boutique stuff, as well.

THE WAREHOUSE, 27 Duke Street, London, W.1. Such high fashion merchandise as Ossie Clark, Janice Wainwright, Pret à Porter, at wholesale prices. Some of it end-of-line new stock, some specially commissioned and made up in The Warehouse's own fabrics.

2. SAVING FACE

JOAN PRICE FACE PLACE, 33 Cadogan Street, S.W.3 Connaught Street, W.2. Sympathetic ladies here will give you impartial advice on what cosmetics and preparations are best for your skin, and will not push you into anything expensive; if you say Mary Quant, Coty, Max Factor are what you can afford, that's okay by them and Estée Lauder and Rubenstein will not be thrust upon you.

CULPEPER. You may be lucky enough to live near one of the branches of this divine herbalist

21 Bruton Street, Berkeley Square, London, W1X 7DA.

9 Flask Walk, Hampstead, London NW3 1HJ.

14 Bridewell Alley, Norwich, NR2 1AQ.

25 Lion Yard, Cambridge, CB2 3NA.

If not, you can now order from them by post, so wherever you live you can cosset yourself with things natural — milk of white violets, mountain water lotion, lemon verbena bath essence, even buy dried elder flowers to make your own astringent lotion. Just reading their list makes you feel prettier — and what's more, the prices are reasonable. Send for your order-form and price-list to:—

Culpeper Ltd, Hadstock Road, Linton, Cambridge, CB1 6NJ.

All their products and all details are on the list.

Feed Your Face by Dian Dincin Buchman, Duckworth, £1.25. A fascinating book, full of recipes for making your own cosmetics; mix your own acne-cure, make astringent with cucumbers, give yourself a facial with honey or oatmeal or yogurt. How to use herbs and flowers to improve your health and skin — plus what you should eat to keep your face looking good, like brewer's yeast for keeping away wrinkles!

Lotions and Potions, edited by Gwynedd Lloyd, 35p inclusive of postage and packing. One of the many interesting publications to be had from The National Federation of Women's Institutes, 39 Eccleston Street, London, SW1 9NT. This pamphlet is a collection of traditional herbal recipes handed down from generation to generation — how to make preparations for your face and hands, remedies and infusions for practically nothing, and using natural ingredients.

Mother Nature's Beauty Cupboard, by Donna Lawson, Robert Hale & Co. Another lovely have-a-go collection of recipes for beauty, some down-to-earth, some exotic.

3. ALL YOU NEED IS A GOOD CUT

THE SCALP AND HAIR

HOSPITAL OF THE INSTITUTE OF TRICHOLOGISTS, 228 Stockwell Road, London, S.W.9. Tel: 01-733-2056. Professional service from experts. They will not advise you on the 'phone, quite rightly insisting that they have to see individual hair problems to treat them properly. But if you write to them, they will give you the name of your nearest qualified trichologist. Best thing is to go and see them. Consultation costs £2.25. Subsequent treatments range between £1.40 and £1.80, and their recommended lotions and shampoos cost about 40p. Worth knowing that these prices are about a *third* of what you would pay at a glossier establishment.

CULPEPER once again, for the best in natural products and the cheapest way of doing it; do-your-own-henna, marvellous shampoos, rinses and conditioners made of nettles, rosemary and bay. Order form and price-list from:—

Culpeper Ltd, Hadstock Road, Linton, Cambridge, CB1 6NJ.

Note that orders under £3.00 excluding postage cannot be handled by mail-order, but you can get a lot for that £3!

CLAIROL, makers of the most widely used home hair-colouring of all sorts will give you advice FREE about semi-permanent rinses, tinting, toners, even highlights. Very comforting to hysterical ladies who've come out the wrong colour! Telephone for help to:—

Joan Clair — 01-845-5541 or write for advice to:—

Joan Clair, Stonefield Way, Ruislip, Middlesex, HA4 0JN.

L'OREAL run their own school of hair colouring, using their well-known products. You can apply to be a model for the students and for the amazing price of £2 you can get any sort of colouring done, including highlights. You have to be interviewed first though; you've got to have the right sort of hair, *and* the right sort of personality — patience, above all, as you are there as a demonstration for students, and there will be pauses for explanation. Be prepared to give up a whole morning or afternoon. The preparations are actually made there, the whole process carefully supervised; if you're suitable you can be one of their regulars. Phone or write for an interview to:

Pamela Goff, L'Oreal School, 18 Bruton Street, London, W.1.

Interviews are between 2 p.m. and 4 p.m. on Thursdays.

AFTER-HOURS HAIRDRESSING. Be a model for junior trainee stylists, but only go to the best.

VIDAL SASSOON. Only the Grosvenor Street salon has modelling nights. Turn up at 6 p.m. on Tuesdays and Wednesdays, and wait your turn. Cutting and blow-dry are *free*. Tinting can be arranged by chatting up the junior who's working on you — then they just charge the cost of the preparation they use.

Or, be a guinea-pig at their school:—

56 Davies Mews, London, W.1. Tel: 01-629-4635. More civilised, as you can book an appointment, but it costs £1.20 for cut, wash and blow-dry, which is still a

quarter of the salon price.

LEONARD, 6 Upper Grosvenor Street, W.1. Tel: 01-629-5757. Model nights are Monday, Tuesday and Wednesday — 6 pm onwards. Just turn up and be prepared to wait — they're very popular. Fifty pence for cut and blow dry by a junior, supervised by stylists. You can book for a junior to do tinting, perming, or high-lighting — all at £1.50.

RICCI BURNS, 94 George Street, W.1. Tel: 01-935-3657. You can actually book an appointment here on model nights, Tuesdays and Wednesdays between 6-8 p.m. Cutting and blow-dry are free. Book well ahead and you can get tinting and perming — if you're lucky.

All juniors are carefully supervised.

4. MINI-MARKETING

Which Magazine is a must for budget-minded people. It comes out once a month and will give you the best buys in all household goods and food — they do the dirty work for you, and trudge from one supermarket to the other and find out what's cheapest and best. Order it from:

Consumers Association, 14 Buckingham Street, London, WC2N 6DS.

WHICH ADVICE CENTRE, 242 Kentish Town Road, Tel: 01-485-9939, London, N.W.5. This is run by the Consumers Association, and its services are free to anyone who calls in (no phone or post advice, I'm afraid). They will help you with information before you go and buy anything — fridge, kettle, T.V., bicycle, whatever. If you've got a lot of queries, you can phone them and arrange an appointment. When you're there you can catch up on back numbers of *Which* and other consumer leaflets.

They are open Tuesday, Wednesday, Friday, Saturday — 10 am - 6 pm Thursday 10 am - 1.30 pm

Making Ends Meet by Elizabeth Gundry, Arrow Family Handbook, 95p. Simple practical guide to managing money. How to budget, save, plan, keep accounts — find out where the money's going, and how to spend it best. Invaluable to people setting up home in inflationary times.

NEW COVENT GARDEN MARKET, 1 Nine Elms Lane, London, S.W.8. Take a strong man with you if you want to buy fruit and veg here — you'll have to buy at least a crate of oranges, or a whole box of avocados, and private cars are not allowed to drive into the market. But on foot you're allowed in before 11 am. You probably won't get quite wholesale prices, (they do know their customers and see you coming), but it's quite a bit cheaper if you want to buy large quantities, and the freshness and quality are superb. Marvellous idea if you're having a party.

NATIONAL ASSOCIATION OF WHOLESALE MARKETS Write to: The Secretary, NAMBA, 3 St. Jude's Avenue, Mapperly, Nottingham and they will give you information about your nearest wholesale markets, and what use you can make of them. It's amazing what you can do if you try.

If you *must* bulk-buy, here are

two firms to write to:

JOHN DRON LTD, Devonshire House, London N8 9SN. They deliver all over the country and can save you a lot of nervous energy. Their catalogue includes household goods, paper goods (things like tissues, disposable nappies, toilet paper), hardware, tea and coffee, cleaning materials, textiles — the list is impressive.

BUY BULK. Send 30p for their catalogue to: Buybulk Ltd, Tunnel Bank Road, Bourne, Lincs. Tel: Bourne 3291. They trade in all sorts of tinned food and groceries, freezer equipment, linens, stationery, light bulbs, things for the car and the garden, brooms, cake-tins, towels, baby clothes — it leaves you breathless.

This firm also have CASH AND CARRY places with huge range of goods; low prices, large car-park, at the following addresses:

BUYBULK LTD, Tunnel Bank Road, Bourne, Lincs, (Mon-Sat 9.00am-5.30 pm Thurs-Fri open until 8 pm.)

BUYBULK LTD, Eastfields Road, Off Dove Fields, Uttoxeter, Staffs, (Mon-Sat, 9 am-5.30 pm. Wed and Fri until 8 pm.)

BUYBULK LTD, Racecourse Road, Pershore, Wors. (Mon-Sat 9 am-5.30 pm. Thurs and Fri open until 8 pm.)

DISCOUNT BUYING AGENCY, 111 South Farm Road, Worthing, Sussex. An establishment which does not only discount but also mail-order, so it is worthwhile contacting if you have to lay out money on big household items like cookers, dishwashers, etc. You get between 10 and 20 per cent off retail prices of nationally known brands.

Where to go for original, cut-price presents? If you think our theory that "money/soap/booze covers just everybody" is a bit of a bore, you could try:

CULPEPER is a marvellous source of unusual and reasonable presents, and what's more you can do it by post. There's a wild herb collection in a presentation box for 75p, a basket of spices from the West Indies together with a recipe leaflet for £1.25, pot-pourri, pomanders, sleep-cushions, oils and essences — a most seductive collection of sure-fire successful gifts, stronger on imagination than money. Send for the list to: Culpeper Ltd., Hadstock Road, Linton, Cambridge, CB1 NJ.

CRABTREE AND EVELYN, 34 Savile Row, London, W.1. Why buy your man Eau Sauvage when for half the price you can have him smelling deliciously of East Indian Lemons and Spices? Just one of the many ravishing colognes made by Crabtree and Evelyn; lovely original smells in beautiful old-fashioned packaging. The address above is not a shop, but if you write they will send you a list of all their soaps, colognes and lotions, together with the name of your nearest stockist. (Enclose a large stamped addressed envelope.)

Pot-pourris and Other Fragrant Delights by Jacqueline Heriteau, Lutterworth, £2.90. How to make your own perfumed presents; lavender bags, herb pillows, scents for burning to make rooms smell lovely and lots more ideas. Plus what to grow to put into your "fragrant delights" — which roses have the most scent, flowers with the most lasting smell, which herbs you'll need.

THE NEAL STREET SHOP, 29 Neal Street, Covent Garden, London, W.C.2. Tel: 01-240-0136. Send for their attractive broadsheet for examples of the cheap, pretty things they sell which make ideal presents. They specialise in goods direct from China — fans, jewellery, flower-paintings, baskets, bamboo, feathers — all sorts of enchanting gifts. They operate a small mail-order business, but this has to be very restricted to a small selection as the stock changes so often. Well worth a visit if you're in the area.

WAREHOUSE, 39 Neal Street, Covent Garden, London, W.C.2. Tel: 01-240-0931. While you're in the district, this is another treasure trove. Hundreds of ethnic presents from all over the world — Peru, India, China, Afghanistan. They too operate mail-order trading, but only of staple items because of uncertain deliveries. Don't feel deprived if you live out of London; there are two similar shops;

The Bristol Guild of Applied Art, 68 Park Street, Bristol and *Rossiter,* 40 Broad Street, Bath.

Homebound Craftsmen, 25A Holland Street, London, W.8. Soft toys for presents for small children made by the old and the disabled, and sold at reasonable prices.

5. THE FREEZER MYTH

BIRDS-EYE run a nationwide "freezer line" service, Mondays to Fridays between 9 a.m. and 5 p.m. Use this advisory service for any enquiries about thawing, freezing, packing and storage and you will get help from a team of home economists. The number to ring is Walton-on-Thames 24071.

Birds-Eye publish an excellent book, complete with recipes and freezing techniques. It is free but send an 11p. stamp for postage and packing to: Mar-Pat Mailings Ltd., Dept 539 The Old Pines, Epsom, Surrey.

BEJAM, one of the largest freezer centre firms, publish a monthly newspaper called "Bejam News" which gives you a lot of information amongst the plugs for the months' best buys and bargains. Send a postal order or cheque for 86p. to cover postage for the year and they will send it to you: *Bejam News,* 161 Fellows Road, Swiss Cottage, London,, N.W.3 36JA.

From the hundreds of books about freezers and how to use them, here are a select few:

Home Freezing by Mary Norwak, Sphere, 40p. Beginners start here. Basic rules of how to use the thing and useful to have for reference.

The Penguin Freezer Cookbook by Helge Rubinstein and Sheila Bush, Penguin, 40p. A book which could well convert you to freezing. A brisk introduction, then a month-by-month guide of what to freeze in its season: pheasant in January, smoked haddock in February, pigeons in March...and on through the year. Lovely recipes — a gastronomic treatment of a chilly subject.

Growing, Freezing and Cooking

by Mary Norwak and Keith Mossman, Sphere, 60p, which seems a logical approach. Growing produce is one of the best reasons for having a freezer, after all.

Step by Step Guide to Home Freezing by Audrey Ellis, Hamlyn, £1.25. A good practical book about how to buy, run, and make the best use of your freezer.

Fresh from the Freezer by Mary Cameron-Smith, Penguin, 45p. Brief, brisk and very much to the point and includes a useful list of manufacturers and distributors of freezers.

Apart from freezer centres, there are speciality foods you can buy:

MARINE ICES. This firm sell delicious ice-creams (rum and butter, peanut crunch, marsala, creme de menthe, to name but a few) fruit sorbets, cassata, pizza — all top quality. You can buy the ice-creams and sorbets in gallon cans (50-60 portions) which is a good idea for school hols and children's parties.

LORIER LTD, 35 Drayton Gardens, London, S.W.10 — Tel: 01-373-6777. They import sorbet from France and will send it to you. The flavours are strawberry, lemon, raspberry, pear, mandarin, passion fruit, prune and greengage. All are made of fresh fruit purée, sugar and egg white — quite superb. A 5-litre box (about 650 scoops) costs about £7. It is guaranteed to keep in your freezer for a year without deteriorating. If you live out of London, you have to order a minimum of 4 boxes.

R. TUCKER — BUTCHERS LTD, 493 Lordship Lane, E. Dul-wich, London, S.E.22. Tel: 693-8374-5208. There are 19 branches of this chain of butchers, and if you get on to their mailing list they will send you a monthly broadsheet of what meat is the best buy for your freezer at the time. Write to them or phone for information.

A list of some freezer centres over the country:—

BEJAM GROUP — S.E. and S. Midlands.

CORDON BLEU — N.W., N. Midlands and Yorkshire.

DALGETY FROZEN FOOD CENTRES — S.E.

SO-COLD SUPERSTORES — Anglia.

BONIMART — London.

MASTER FREEZE FOODS — Scotland.

FREEZER FARE — South East.

6. CUT-PRICE FEASTING

EVENING INSTITUTE CLASSES. Impress your friends by having a go at the super-cook's course, quick and easy entertaining, gourmet cooking, hostess cooking, all sorts of baking and pastry-making, and cookery from every country you can think of — Hungarian, Chinese, French, Scandinavian, Indian, Italian — even English.

NATIONAL FEDERATION OF WOMEN'S INSTITUTES, 39 Eccleston St., London, S.W.1. Some of their useful homespun advice in:

One-point Cooking a pamphlet teaching you how to use only one part of your cooker for the whole meal and save fuel. Twenty pence including postage and packing.

Preservation by Joan Ellis, 35p, includes jam-making, canning, bottling, pickling, chutney — a must if you want to make the most of seasonal produce, especially if you live in the country or have a garden.

Home-made Wines by F. W. Beach, 75p — wine-making for the new recruit; basic principles, ingredients and variations, with chapters on the equipment you need, problems that crop up, and the joys of tasting. Send for any of these to the above address; the prices include package and posting.

Two rather depressing titles, but both books are full of good sense, economical ideas, and nice recipes:

The Pauper's Cookbook by Jocasta Innes, Penguin, 60p.

Left-over For Tomorrow by Marika Hanbury-Tenison, Penguin, 55p.

Buy Wisely, Eat Well by Beryl Gould-Marks, Faber, £1.10. Good cooking on a restricted budget, and full of imaginative recipes for cheaper cuts of meat, and those nourishing pulses they keep telling us to eat.

Food for Free by Richard Mabey, Fontana, £1.75. The ultimate in economy. The book is great fun and fascinating. You may not be lucky enough to find a truffle on your country outings, but you'll certainly learn from this book how and where to find mushrooms, sorrel to make delicious soup, berries, nuts, all sorts of edible wild plants.

The Penguin Book of Home Brewing and Wine-making by W. H. T. Tayleur, 50p. A lovely read, and all you need to know about making beer at home, and masses of information about every aspect of wine-making.

Poor Cook by Susan Campbell and Caroline Conran, Macmillan, £2.50.

The Four Seasons Cook Book by Margaret Costa, Sphere, 75p. This superb cookery writer takes you through the year using fresh, seasonal ingredients; spring lamb, summer strawberries, autumn pears and plums, winter root vegetables. Quite the nicest approach to cooking; what's in season not only tastes better, it's cheaper.

A Book of Mediterranean Food, 45p.

French Provincial Cooking, £1.25.

French Country Cooking, 60p.

Summer Cooking, 70p. — all published by Penguin, written by Elizabeth David. The classics, and no cook should be without them. And if you wince as you pour a bottle of 90p. Beaujolais type plonk into the pot, just stop and consider what "coq au vin" would cost you in a restaurant.

The Evening Standard Cookbook by Delia Smith, 95p. One of the nicest cookery books around by one of the nicest T.V. cooks. Delia Smith's recipes never seem to go wrong, and she has delicious ideas which don't cost much money — probably because she uses a lot of country recipes, and quite a few traditional English dishes like steak and kidney pudding and Lancashire Hotpot. We can promise that her four-star Shepherd's Pie and Apple Nut Crumble are quite sensational. Marvellous, mouth-watering old-fashioned puddings

— just reading about them makes you feel fat, but it's all very seductive.

Cheap Chow by Kenneth Lo, Elm Tree Books, £2.95. Shows how budget-conscious Chinese make ½lb meat stretch to feed six. Sensibly westernised recipes, too.

7. EATING ETHNIC

Time Out magazine, 25p. — aptly sub-titled "London's Living Guide", and no Londoner who wants to go out and not spend a fortune can afford to be without it. Every week it's crammed with details of off-beat concerts, free films at libraries and museums, film-clubs where you can see classic films at low prices, fringe-theatres, and the latest finds in cheap eating places. They now have a page called "Sell-out" which gives you news on bargains, jumble-sales, new markets — every aspect of cheap living.

Egon Ronay Guide to Transport Cafes by Crane Fruehauf, Seymour, 95p. This is the nearest thing we've got to the French "routier" way of eating. Cheap nosh all over the country; meat and two veg in Felixstowe for 34p. and a caff in Husband's Bosworth in Leicestershire where you can get fry-ups and grills from 23p. to £1.20 — friendly service, fresh flowers, and warmed plates to boot. Super book if you're planning a cheap driving holiday in England.

AA Guide to Guesthouses, Farmhouses, and Inns — pretty stodgy but very useful, as it includes only *low-cost* meals and accommodation.

The New Egon Ronay Dunlop Guide £3.20 — the usual guide to hotels, restaurants, and inns in Great Britain, but the new edition includes 700 bargain restaurants and weekend breaks.

A Guide to Chinese Eating by Kenneth Lo, Phaidon Press, £2.95. Definitive guide to telling your Chow Mein from your Chop Suey.

Cheap Eats in London by Susan Campbell and Alexandra Towle, Penguin, 50p. — where to find the best pizza, Chinese and Indian food, spaghetti houses — very useful and nicely presented.

Fuel Food by Mike Bygrave and Joan Goodman, Wildwood Press, £1.25 — where to get great meals in London for £1.25 and under. A good collection with things like fish and chip shops, kebab houses, the usual ethnic and vegetarian havens, and some off-beat suggestions like an eel and pie shop, and a "creperie" — lovely filling Breton Pancakes, a meal in themselves, for as little as 60p.

Timing your meal can be tricky if you want to take in a film or play the same evening. *THE MERMAID THEATRE* (Puddle Dock, London, EC4) sensibly serve an excellent three-course dinner in their restaurant before the play and it's all in the price of the ticket.

Good Nouveau Poor tip for free tickets, incidentally, is the *BBC TICKET UNIT,* Broadcasting House, London, W.1. If you write to them, enclosing a stamped addressed envelope, you can get tickets absolutely free for comedy shows with live audiences, some T.V. programmes, and best of all, top-class concerts with the greatest orchestras and soloists at the BBC concert hall in Maida Vale, London, W.9. If you don't live in London, get in touch with your local BBC centre, as quite a few concerts come from Manchester, Cardiff, Birmingham and other cities.

ALMOST FREE THEATRE, Rupert Street, London, W.1. Tel: 01-485-6224 — usually somewhat controversial plays, well-produced and acted. Performed at lunch-time and in the evening, and you pay what you can afford.

THE KING'S HEAD, 115 Upper Street, London, N.1. Tel: 01-226-1916. One of the best of the many mushrooming pub theatres. Eat and drink while you watch star performers in super productions. You don't have to have dinner there, but for £3 for both the meal and the play it's pretty good value for a night out.

EMBASSY THEATRE, Centre School of Speech and Drama, 64 Eton Avenue, London, N.W.3. Send 50p. for postage and you will be sent information of productions performed at certain times of the year by final year students at the school. Tickets are 50p., and you could well see stars of the future in Chekhov, Shakespeare, Pinter — they only perform the best.

THE VANBRUGH THEATRE CLUB, Malet Street, London, W.C.1. Tel: 01-580-7982. A year's membership is £1.05, and here you see the best of RADA's students in a wide range of plays, excellently produced. Tickets are 40p in the evening, 20p for matinees.

Letts publish three attractive handbooks at 60p each.
Eat and Sleep in London — The Good Value Guide.
What's Free in London — See The City Without Expense.
Where to buy in London — From Jewels to Jellied Eels.

8. IF YOU'RE VERY GOOD, DARLING, MUMMY WILL GIVE YOU A NICE CARD-BOARD BOX...

MOTHERCARE BY POST. The mail-order side of the nation-wide chain of stores. Everything from maternity clothes, through nappies, prams, baby-clothes, toys — and now clothes for children up to ten years old. The things are attractive and practical, and they keep their prices as low as possible. The easy-to-handle catalogue includes a list of all their hundreds of branches if you would rather shop personally. Send for it to: Mothercare by Post, Cherry Tree Road, Watford, WD2 5SH.

ARGOS DISTRIBUTORS LTD, Argos House, The Hyde, London NW9 5AL. One of the biggest discount houses, with 13 London branches, and 30 all over the rest of the country. They say their very low prices come from saving on rent and rates, using computerised warehousing and bulk purchasing. Whatever the reason they are *cheap* and you will certainly save money on all that initial outlay stuff — cellular blankets, cot, play-pen, high chair — and later on their toys are sold much more cheaply than the same makes in other shops. The drill is to send for the catalogue, choose what you need, then find your nearest Argos distributor in the list at the back of the book.

Exchange and Mart. Comes out every Thursday and has a special section devoted to Baby and Nursery. Some second-hand things.

Nursery World is another weekly worth buying for the small ads: in Baby Things for Sale.

BABY SCALE HIRE, 61, Lilford Road, S.E.5. Tel: 01-274-8762 and

GUARDIAN BABY SCALES LTD, 45 Holloway Road, N.7. Tel: 01-602-6105. Both these firms hire out baby scales and deliver in the London area.

Bibi's Cookbook by Barbara Griggs, Allen and Unwin, £2.95. The only book of its kind, based on the author's own experience of what nutrition babies need and how to make them really enjoy their food.

Making Toys, ed Ron Bloomfield, B.B.C. Publication, £1.20 (plus 22p postage). Lovely illustrated paperback for parents new to toy-making, full of instructions on how to make attractive, *safe* toys for very little cost.

Making Soft Toys, Gillian Lockwood, 95p.

Making Clothes for Young Children, Gillian Lockwood, 75p. Two useful books by Studio Vista.

Making Things for Children by Katie Dyson, Octopus Press, 95p. This is full of good ideas for things you can do yourself and save pounds. Not only baby clothes and knitting patterns, but nursery accessories, rag dolls, crocheted rugs, patchwork quilts and lots more.

NATIONAL FEDERATION OF WOMEN'S INSTITUTES. They have lots of pamphlets for 20p each on making lovely things like teddy bears, glove puppets, rag dolls, and cuddly animals galore. Send for them to 39, Eccleston Street, S.W.1.

9. THE FLEXIBLE, ADAPTABLE, SWITCHAROUND HOME...

Buying a House by L. E. Vickers, Penguin Handbook, 50p. All the financial and legal aspects of house buying. Very clear, sharp, and full of warnings! Tells you everything about surveyors, solicitors, building societies, raising money: mortgages of every sort — endowment, local authority, insurance company — the lot.

The Penguin Guide to Insurance by George Willman, Penguin Handbook, 40p. Every variety you need; life, accident, sickness, car, house-holders, fire, theft — you name it!

Help Yourself by Mavis Nicholson, Coronet, 50p. In this jam-packed little book is every public service, organisation, what have you, and includes jolly good sections on all things legal, including house-buying and insurance.

THE NATIONAL HEATING CENTRE, 34 Mortimer Street, London, W.1. Tel: 01-380-3238. There is an exhibition permanently on show here of all sorts of heating and a library of leaflets. They don't give advice on the 'phone, but for £1 you can have a consultation on your individual problems or an answer to a written enquiry.

THE BUILDING CENTRE, 26 Store Street, London, W.C.1. Tel: 01-637-1022. Marvellous place with permanent displays of everything that goes into building and decorating — bricks, tiles, flooring, heating, bathrooms, and double glazing. They give impartial advice, and appropriate leaflets. You can get leaflets by post on the subject you're interested in by writing to Mr Peachey (Enquiries) at the above address — just enclose 10p in stamps.

THE HOME IMPROVEMENT CENTRE has no less than 500 centres all over the country, with displays and people to advise. For the official address list write to: National Federation of Builders and Plumbers' Merchants, High Holborn House, 52/54 High Holborn, London, WC1 V6SP. These centres tell you not only how to plan your home improvements, but how to finance them. Two books on central heating:

Choosing Your Central Heating, Hamlyn £1.25. Glossy, quite fun, but very informative: installation, maintenance, thermostats, boilers, what sort of fuel...

Central heating-Consumers Association Guide (publishers of Which) £2.15. 14 Buckingham Street, London, WC2N 6DS.

Keeping Warm at Half the Cost by Phil Townsend and John Colesby, Prism Press, £1.25. From bookshops or you can send for it enclosing 15p postage to: Prism Press, Stable Court, Chalmington, Dorchester, Dorset. Tells you the basic principles of the dreaded heat loss, and ways of beating it: insulation of roofs, walls and floors; double glazing; how to stop nasty draughts, and how to cut those fuel bills.

Hammer it Home by Tony Wilkins, BBC Publication, 50p. Smashing little production, like all BBC publications. Straightforward, clear lay-out with diagrams and illustrations; perfect home-decorating for beginners.

Budget Brighteners for the Home, Golden Hands Publication, £1.25. This hardback book is fantastic value. Not only painting and decorating, but lots of clever, creative, and inexpensive ways of beautifying your home. Like face-lifts for old furniture — strip it, polish it, stain it, paint it! Upholstery, picture-framing, restoring the glow to old copper and brass, making table-lamps, useful hints on wise buying, and all about the tools you'll need and how to use them.

Flat Broke by Barbara Chandler, Pitman, £2.95. Sub-titled "A Guide to Almost Free Furnishing"! Gives inexpensive ways of equipping your first flat, and some off-beat suppliers.

Floodlight is the ILEA guide to adult-education classes, and in it you'll find all the courses you can take in home-decorating — wood stripping, upholstery, loose-cover making, furniture restoration, and lots more. Your local library will have a copy of Floodlight, or you can get your own by sending 5p. in stamps and a stamped addressed envelope to: G.L.C. Information Bureau, County Hall, London, S.E.1. Other parts of the country — you can get details of your local evening and day classes from your local County Education Officer. The cost for a year's tuition is kept as low as possible, and the teaching is excellent.

The Complete Guide to London's Antique Street Markets by Jeremy Cooper, Thames & Hudson. Jolly book full of maps, how-to-get there, opening times, dealers, personalities — even whether you can get on-the-spot food, drink and entertainment while you rummage around. Having found your junk, two useful title books:

Restoring Junk by Suzanne Beedell, Macdonald & Janes, £1.95.

Converting Junk by Fiona Windrum, Macdonald, £1.50, among many ideas, "Convert your simple divan into a glamorous four-poster"!

Two smashing junk places:

AUSTINS, 11/13 Peckham Rye, London, S.E.15 — the biggest and probably still the best. Floor upon floor of furniture from antique to plain grotty, bric-a-brac, carpets, a vast depository where all the dealers go.

SECOND-HAND CITY, Methodist Church, North End Road, London, W.14. Cheap solid furniture, ideal for stripping and re-painting yourself.

HABITAT. The well-known and lovely Conran designs can now be obtained by mail-order. Send for the catalogue (include 30p. for postage) to: Habitat, Wallingford, Oxfordshire.

Among the household goods and furniture, you will find pages devotes to their *Basic Range;* super design at lowest possible prices. Things like hand-woven Indian cotton rugs; stainless steel dishwater-proof cutlery; dark brown Bistro casseroles;

thick soft blue blankets, and white Terry towels.

Rochford's Houseplants for Everyone by Thomas Rochford (himself) and Richard Gorer, Faber, 80p.

Houseplants by Thomas Rochford, published by the Royal Horticultural Society, 70p. These are both very dependable, coming as they do from the horse's mouth. If you want something glossier:

The Complete Indoor Gardener, Pan, £3.95. Not only indoor plants, but how to grow things from pips, vegetables without a garden, window boxes. Very attractive and comprehensive book, full of inspiring ideas.

London Shopping Guide by Elsie Burch Donald, Penguin, 75p could go in under almost any chapter heading because it tells you where to buy everything and anything from the one-third off book remainders to the best furniture and carpet discount warehouses, taking in every possible service on the way. If you live in London, occasionally visit London, or just want to take advantage of London mail-order services, buy it.

10. DON'T BUY IT, GROW IT

Basic Gardening by Alan Gemmel, Penguin, 60p. The firm and fatherly advice of one of the regulars of the BBC's "Gardeners' Question Time" in a first-class ABC of gardening for the beginner; he covers everything from tools and soil, through shrubs, flowers, veg, fruit, and even house-plants.

The Small Garden by C. E.

Lucas Phillips, Pan, 95p. One of the best books on general gardening principles, with good ideas on how to plan your garden.

Gardeners' Question Time. 100 selected questions and answers from the famous BBC team of experts. Two books, 25p and 40p — BBC Publications.

Window-Box Gardening by Xenia Field, Blandford Press, £1.75. How to get the best out of window-boxes, with flowers, foliage, and winter colour; salads and herbs, too, and what to put in tubs, pots, hanging baskets and any other containers.

THE DESIGN CENTRE publish an excellent book by Peter Shepherd on how to plan a garden.

Two books from the Royal Horticultural Society:
Growing Plants for Flower Arrangements by Sybil Emberton, 70p. Don't be put off by the "arrangement" bit; valuable advice about shrubs to grow which will give you flowers and leaves for cutting all the year round, and
The Vegetable Garden Displayed £1.80. The whole digging, sowing and harvesting scene, with lots of illustrations.

The Complete Vegetable Grower by W. E. Shewell-Cooper, Faber, 60p. Heavy going, but good if you're going into it really seriously and have an allotment, or lots of space.

Mr. Smith's Vegetable Garden, BBC Publication, 60p. Lovely Geoffrey Smith from the T.V. series tells beginners just what to grow. Veg are in alphabetical order, it's attractive, easy to follow, with pretty black and white drawings.

Two pamphlets from the National Federation of Women's Institutes:
Food from the Small Garden by Pamela Sutherland, 20p. and
Growing and Cooking Unusual Vegetables by Joan Roulston and Anne Harris. Twenty-two varieties with clear instructions and a list of seed stockists.

Survival Gardening by Edward Hyams, John Murray, £2.75. Sub-titled "How to grow vegetables, fruit, herbs, wine, and tobacco in your garden or allotment" — what more could you ask?"

The Two-Hour Garden by Alexander Dingwall Main and Ian Dougill, Corgi, £1.95. A very attractive book based on the *Sunday Times* series on how to have a productive and colourful garden on only two hours' work a week. They give you a work-plan schedule, and it's full of lovely, well-designed illustrations.

Grow Your Own Vegetables (Complete Money Saving Guide), Phoebus, 85p. "350 square yards of good land will provide a year's vegetables for a family of three adults," says the blurb. And *that's* the size of an average suburban garden.

KHAN'S NURSERY, The Herb Farm, Broad Oak Road, Canterbury. Send for their catalogue of unusual vegetables like globe artichokes, peppers, aubergines, fennel — they send lovely healthy plants by post.

E. AND A. EVETS, Ashfield Herb Nursery, Hinstock, Market Drayton, Shropshire. Highly recommended for their superb culinary, scented, and decorative herbs, which they send so beautifully packed that they arrive with the dew still on them.

ROTOCROP LTD, 848, Brighton Road, Purley, Surrey, CR2 2UP. They have had the Design Council Award for their "Accelerator" compost bin. You can send for it — a quick, clean method of keeping a supply of compost going.